Your Prayers Are Always Answered

Your Prayers
Are Always Answered

by Alexander Lake

GILBERT PRESS, INC.

Distributed by Julian Messner, Inc.

Published by Gilbert Press, Inc.
A subsidiary of Julian Messner, Inc.
8 West 40th Street, New York 18

© Copyright 1956 by Alexander Lake

Published simultaneously in Canada
by the Copp Clark Company, Ltd.

Library of Congress Catalog Card No.: 56–6791

Eighth Printing, 1963

For my two
MOTHERS
Jennie Stephens Lake
and
Edna Hawn Lawn
—*Their children call them blessed.*

Publisher's Note

Every story in this book is true. Names and descriptive facts have been altered in some instances to protect the privacy of the persons involved.

How

Your Prayers Are Always Answered

came to be written

IN 1910, when I was seventeen, the South African colonies joined to become the Union of South Africa. Louis Botha was appointed National Premier by the King of England. The question of a native policy for the new Union was vital and pressing, and Botha, and other prominent South Africans such as Generals Jan Smuts and Christian De Wet, occasionally came to the Johannesburg home of my missionary father, Dr. John G. Lake, for advice.

These men always knelt and prayed before starting discussions, and they closed each meeting with a prayer of thanks. Sometimes they'd sit for a while, telling stories of answers to prayer. Some of the answers were so remarkable—and made so deep an impression on me—that I began a life-long hobby of collecting prayer stories.

Whenever—anywhere in the world—I hear of some outstanding answer to prayer, I check the story; interview all concerned; dig out the drama connected with it; write detailed notes and file them away.

From a collection of more than 2,000 such stories—all remarkable, fascinating and inspiring—I selected those that seemed to me to have the simplicity, directness, and the human and spiritual qualities so needed by people of this seemingly chaotic and insecure world of today.

Contents

Your Prayers Are Always Answered

I WAS once told of a farmer named Du Bois in French Equatorial Africa, who'd lost everything he owned when the desert encroached on his fertile acres. His situation seemed utterly hopeless, yet he prayed in faith. His neighbors, equally overwhelmed, fled the area, but because of faith in God, Du Bois stayed.

Within a month, poisonous snakes swarmed into his acres, and for a time it looked as if he and his family would be forced to flee for their lives. Du Bois prayed again. Soon he learned to handle cobras safely, and within two years was earning a comfortable income selling venom to be used in making anti-snake-bite serum.

I have notes on many such unusual prayer stories, but the story of the Fernalds, for whom God kindled a flame, is for me the most inspiring.

God Kindled the Flame

IN MARCH 1945, John and Jessie Fernald, both in their fifties, stood almost ankle-deep in mud near the center of a three-acre field on southern Oregon's coastal strip. Their heads were bowed against driving rain. Around them, like drenched white bones, daffodil bulbs lay scattered everywhere, washed to the surface of the ground by the storm.

When the rain had begun seventeen days ago, tender green shoots from sixty thousand growing bulbs had been inches high. John and Jessie, although they'd never before grown daffodils, had invested almost everything they'd owned in planting stock. There'd been moderate rain all winter, and the crop seemed assured. Then had come this prolonged cloudburst—thirty-four inches of rain in seventeen days. With hoes and shovels, they'd worked desperately to drain off the flood. Now the crop lay ruined beyond salvage.

Holding his wife's hand, and with eyes clouded with worry, John said, "It's a bitter blow, Jessie."

"It's a time to pray, John," she said. "We've neglected God's direction long enough."

"There's nothing left to pray about."

John's sense of defeat had sunk deep, and Jessie's throat was tight with compassion. She tried gently to withdraw her fingers, but John clung to them. Hand-in-hand, he led her a hundred yards to the driftwood-strewn ocean beach. They stared out over tumultuous waters, watching the great waves

14

thunder down on the sands, throwing spume high to be snatched by the wind and flung into their faces.

They were too weary and discouraged to talk, but each knew that the other was thinking of how on a balmy summer day two years before, while on vacation from their eastern Ontario farm, they'd first seen this oceanside acreage. The calm blue sea had fascinated them. Wildflowers grew everywhere. The air had been quiet and still. They'd thought of this place as a dream come true. They'd bought on impulse, selling their Ontario place by mail. They had never gone back.

Both were remembering how they'd planned to grow vegetables for a living, and how disappointed they'd been when they learned that the nearest city large enough to offer a market was more than one hundred miles away. Then, to their dismay, the near-perfect weather had given way to damp morning fogs and afternoons of high winds. Almost before they knew it, winter had come with more than one hundred inches of rain.

They'd soon decided that they'd reached a land of few opportunities. Most of their neighbors accepted poverty as a normal condition. A year passed while John made futile attempts to get work. Savings seemed to melt away. Then someone had told them about daffodils, and in desperation they'd invested almost their last dollar. Now they'd lost even that.

Still without speaking, John gathered an armful of driftwood and carried it to the small unpainted house on the edge of the daffodil field. He knelt before the fireplace, arranged the brine-soaked sticks in a pyramid over red coals, and watched flames begin to lick upward through the sizzling, steaming pile.

"Driftwood," he said hopelessly. "Worthless driftwood—exactly what we'll be now."

He got no answer from his wife, and turned to look at her. Her eyes were closed in prayer. Abruptly, the fire crackled with tiny explosions, and thin pencils of blue flame spurted here and there from the surfaces of the small wet logs.

She said, "Look, John—the blue flames!"

"Yes. Ocean salts in the wood turned to gas by the heat," he said. Then impatiently: "You've seen it lots of times."

"Yes, John. But this time, that blue is an answer to prayer."

"A what?"

"I was praying that God show us the best way out of our troubles, and those beautiful flames sprang to life. I *know* they're an answer."

"We can't eat blue flames. What's the answer?"

"I don't quite know yet, John, but it's there. It'll come clear, and work out."

John stood silent for a moment, then went into the next room to change his clothes. Jessie watched the fire. Again and again, the blue pencils thinned, spread, flickered, faded and died only to flare up once more with tinges of yellow and green. Jessie's spirit expanded with a surge of faith. Heaviness left her heart. She knew all would be well although she couldn't yet grasp the message of the flames.

Her skirt began to steam. She turned from the fire, but paused a moment and said softly:

"Dear God, open my mind and heart so I can understand Your message." Then she went to the bedroom to change to dry clothes.

When I interviewed Jessie Fernald in San Diego three years later, she said:

"That night while John and I sat before the fire talking over our problems, I understood God's answer. A batch of damp driftwood had just been heaped on the glowing coals.

Suddenly a fagot blazed brightly, and again, the flame was blue.

"John said, 'Makes me think of Christmas lights.'

"His words filled me with joy . . . warm, sweet and exciting. Tears rolled down my cheeks. John, bewildered and unhappy, asked, 'What in the world's the matter, Jessie?'

"Half-laughing, half-crying, I said: 'My prayer. I know the answer, John. When you said *Christmas lights* just now, I thought of *Christmas fires*. Of logs burning on Christmas hearths—flames of blue, red and orange. Green flames, yellow flames, flames of every color.' Because of a lump in my throat, I stopped speaking, closed my eyes and said silently: 'Thank you, God. Thank you.'

"John was looking at me as if I were crazy. I smiled and said, 'The driftwood, John. The beach is covered with it— long windrows of it. It's there for us to use. We can cut it into Christmas logs—small ones for small fireplaces. They'll sell everywhere.'

"John said: 'Wait a minute, Jessie. Be practical. Only a few of the logs burn blue. We'd need a power saw. Transportation would eat up profits. Wood's heavy to ship. How would we . . . ?'

" 'Hush, John. Remember chemistry class in high school? Remember the time we experimented making pyrotechnic displays? We made all kinds of colored fires. Remember?'

"John's eyes began to match mine. 'Sure I remember,' he said. 'We used salts. I forget which ones. Let's see . . . strontium nitrate burned red, didn't it?'

"I nodded. 'And I think barium chlorate burned green. Oh, John!'

" 'Now, Jessie. Keep calm,' John said. 'The thing's not practical. Anyway, we've no money to stake us until we perfect the Christmas log idea.'

"He began pacing the floor. I said, 'Don't you tell *me* to keep calm, John Fernald. You're the excited one.'

"John ignored me. 'Let's drive to Portland in the morning, Jessie, and dig up some chemistry information.'

" 'John! Portland's three hundred miles from here.'

"John smiled. 'I admit I think you have a swell idea, Jessie,' he said. Then added, 'but there's a lot to work out, and I don't see . . .'

" 'Well, dear, God will help us work it out,' I said. 'Let's get to bed now so we can make an early start in the morning.'

"Two days later we returned from Portland with formulas for red, blue, green, yellow, mauve and purple fires. But we'd had money enough to buy the ingredients for one formula only, and we'd chosen the red. In a 120-gallon hogshead, we mixed strontium nitrate, potassium chlorate, alcohol and water. John took a bucksaw to the beach and cut twenty sixteen-inch fireplace logs from a washed-up redwood limb. We made a ceremony of putting them into the mixture in the barrel. We piled scrap iron on the wood to keep it submerged. Then we looked at one another questioningly. 'What now?' I asked.

" 'The logs should soak in this solution for at least a month,' John said. 'Then they'll have to dry for about another month. Then, if they burn as colorfully as we hope they will, we'll buy or build tanks for the other colors. We'll have to find a market for our logs. I'd say we'll do well to be operating profitably by next Christmas—nine months from now. We have about fifteen dollars. How're we going to live in the meantime?'

" 'I don't know, John. But I'm not worried. God will help us with that problem too.'

"As we prayed that evening, John said, simply: 'Please, Lord, show us the way.'

"About a week later, Mr. Angelo Rossi, mayor of San Francisco, who was also one of that city's leading florists, stopped for lunch at a roadside restaurant near our place. He asked the proprietor:

" 'Who owns that fern-covered hillside down the highway?'

"The proprietor told him we did, and a little later, Mr. Rossi stopped at our driveway and said:

" 'The recent heavy rains have given those ferns up there a wonderful growth. If you'd care to cut, bundle and ship them to us—freight charges collect—we'll buy all you can send.'

"We accepted his offer gratefully, and the ferns brought us more than one hundred dollars the first month. I sent some samples of wild huckleberry branches, and Rossi's agreed to buy quantities of them. To another florist, we sent a small potted five-finger fern. He ordered three hundred, and sent a truck to pick them up.

"On May first, we took the logs from the solution and stacked them so air could circulate among them. On June first we laid our first log on the fire and stood tense, waiting for the blaze to catch. Tears came to our eyes as lovely red flames flickered along the log's length, then burned high. Our experiment was successful. True, there was lots of smoke, but the smoke was beautiful too, and we learned to control it later by reducing the potassium chlorate in the solution.

"And now we prayed for a market for our logs. Again, a miracle. We'd given six of the logs to an auto court about twenty miles up the highway. They'd put one in their fireplace one evening when a chain-store executive from Denver was a guest at the auto court. He became fascinated with the possibilities of colored fires from real logs. He came and looked over our set-up, liked our ideas, and stayed long enough to help us work out costs on a larger program. Then he agreed to buy all the logs we could turn out, at a fair profit to us.

"He intended to sell the logs at retail in his own stores, in bundles of six. But before he was able to do that, he arranged to sell our idea to one of the large manufacturers of pressed fireplace logs. We were well paid for our rights in the project.

"Our venture sounds easy the way I tell it now, but actually, John and I worked harder than we'd ever worked before. We had problems with the solutions for each fire color. John worked out a method of drilling the logs so they soaked up solutions in about ten days instead of a month, and we made a drying room in the garage to speed that part of it.

"We found it best to concentrate on only five colors—red, blue, green, yellow and mauve. And one day a minor explosion taught us to keep sulphur away from chlorate of potassium. Only prayer, you know, could have shown us the path through so many difficulties.

"And we made enough money to build this small home here near San Diego. We sold our Oregon coast farm. We'll not grow rich, but we'll have income from the logs sufficient for our needs.

"Our experiment with the colored fire logs taught us the truth of Luke 18:1—*that men ought always to pray, and not to faint;* and that the full answer to prayer does not always come in a single revelation, but that God reveals His plans for us according to our ability to accept them; that those seeking God's help in a difficult endeavor should pray for understanding. We learned also, that no matter how lacking in opportunities an area may seem, God has placed an abundance there. He will reveal it to us if we ask Him in humility and faith."

*W*HEN *Mrs. Henry (Hank) Fine, of Hollywood, read the manuscript of "God Set Them on the Path," she said: "For some reason, the Damaschs' story reminds me of Fra Giovanni's letter to 'Most Noble Contessina.' "*

The Giovanni letter was written on Christmas Eve, 1513 A. D. Thousands throughout the world read the letter daily as a means of inspiration.

Most Noble Contessina, I salute you:

Forgive an old man's babble. But I am your friend, and my love for you goes deep. There is nothing I can give you which you have not got: but there is much, very much, that, while I cannot give it, you can take. No Heaven can come to us unless our hearts find rest in it today. Take Heaven! No peace lies in the future which is not hidden in this present little instant. Take peace! The gloom of the world is but a shadow. Behind it, yet within our reach, is joy. There is radiance and glory in the darkness, could we but see: and to see, we have only to look. Contessina, I beseech you to look.

Life is so generous a giver, but we, judging its gifts by their covering, cast them away as ugly or heavy or hard. Remove the covering and you will find beneath it a splendor, woven of love, by wisdom, with power. Welcome it, grasp it, and you touch the Angel's hand that brings it to you. Everything we call a trial, a sorrow, or a duty: believe me, that Angel's hand is there; the gift is there, and the wonder of an overshadowing Presence. Our joys too: be not content with them as joys. They, too, conceal diviner gifts. Life is so full of meaning and

21

of purpose, so full of beauty—beneath its covering—that you will find earth but cloaks your heaven. Courage, then, to claim it: that is all! But courage you have: and the knowledge that we are pilgrims together, wending, through unknown country, home.

And so, at this Christmas time, I greet you: not quite as the world sends greetings, but with profound esteem, and with the prayer that for you, now and forever, the day breaks and the shadows flee away.

I have the honor to be your servant, though the least worthy of them.

—Fra Giovanni

God Set Them on the Path

ONE DAY IN April 1947, I flagged down a bus about thirty-five miles east of Barstow on U. S. Highway 66. The day was hot, but the Mojave Desert was beautiful. Greasewood stood dusty and gray on a carpet of yellow wildflowers. The interior of the bus was comparatively cool, and I sank gratefully into a seat behind two desert-bronzed men.

The bus droned into the west as if to meet the setting sun. I paid little attention to conversation around me until one of the men in front of me remarked to his companion:

"There was nothing specific I could ask God for, so I prayed that He'd help me solve my problems in His own way. And He did."

I waited, hoping to hear more, but the man sat in silence. I leaned forward and tapped him on the shoulder, and said, "For years I've been collecting stories about answers to prayer. I overheard what you said just now, and I'm interested."

The man smiled; came back and sat beside me. His name was Ovid Damasch. While he was at college in Germany, his family had lost its money, and he'd come to America, almost penniless. He'd worked hard, and after a few years was operating a small contracting business. He now lived at the foot of the Calico Mountains, with his wife, Hulda, and their six-year-old daughter, Tilde. Damasch told me this story:

"Our baby was born in 1941, when Hulda and I were both

nearing fifty. Tilde was a wonderful thing to happen to us, for we'd given up hope of having children. She was a beautiful, healthy baby, and we centered our lives in her.

"Shortly after Pearl Harbor, a materials shortage forced me out of business, so I got a job as rigger in a Richmond, California, shipyard. Despite discomforts of the wartime housing project, things went well for almost three years. Then Tilde began to fail. She grew listless, didn't smile or talk much, just lay quietly, half awake, half asleep.

"Doctors could find no cause for her condition. She grew weaker. Hulda and I took her from one doctor to another, but none was able to help. One day an old, gray-haired physician—a Dr. Danskin, long retired from practice—saw her as she lay on Hulda's lap in a streetcar, and said:

" 'Your baby is very ill, Madam. If you want her well again, get her out of this climate. She needs sunlight; she needs to be bathed in sunlight. Take her to the Mojave Desert.'

"The kind old gentleman came to our house that evening and examined Tilde thoroughly. 'Another month may be too late,' he warned. 'Take this baby to the desert at once, and keep her there until she's well.'

" 'We haven't that kind of money,' I told him. 'We haven't saved much of anything from my wages.'

" 'Draw your pay, fill your car with groceries, drive far into the Mojave, find an abandoned shack—there're lots of them—and give this child a chance to live.'

" 'Can I get a job in the desert?' I asked.

" 'I doubt it.'

" 'How'll we live?'

" 'Pray.'

" 'For a job?'

" 'No,' the doctor said. 'Don't tell God how to help you.

Put yourself in His hands. Tell Him you need His aid—then wait. Wait without worry or impatience. He'll answer.'

" 'I haven't prayed for a long time,' I said.

" 'Well, grow up,' the old man replied.

"Hulda said: 'Ovid, I've been praying for quite a while. I think that's the reason Dr. Danskin's here.' Tears sprang into her eyes. 'Let's go to the desert, dear,' she said.

"I had a feeling that things were out of my hands. 'Well, okay,' I said. 'I can always come back and get my job again.'

" 'You won't have to come back,' the doctor said. 'And don't forget that I'll be praying, too.'

"Dr. Danskin seemed utterly confident, and I felt a surge of faith. After he'd gone, Hulda and I knelt beside our baby's bed. I said something like this:

" 'Dear God, we believe that You have set our feet on this strange path. Alone, we could not travel it because of uncertainty and fear. Please hold our hands in Yours. We'll follow wherever You lead.'

"When we got up from our knees, Hulda and I were both crying a bit. I took her in my arms. Then we looked down at Tilde. She was sleeping soundly.

"Two days later we got into our beaten-up Ford and headed for San Bernardino. My pay check, added to our small hoard of savings, gave us a little more than a hundred and ten dollars.

"At San Bernardino I went into a chain store and bought about fifty dollars' worth of canned goods. As the clerk put them into cartons, the store manager came up and asked a few questions. Then he said: 'I'm going to give you a discount on these purchases. We don't often get fifty-dollar orders.'

"The discount wasn't big, but it strengthened my faith, and as we entered Joshua National Forest, I said to Hulda,

'I left any doubts I may have had, back in that grocery store, Hulda.'

"She said: 'I wonder that I've forgotten to pray through all these years, Ovid. Mother and Father taught us to pray about everything.'

"We passed through Barstow as the sun dipped behind the hills. A cool wind came with the dusk and washed the heat of the day away. In the east, a reflected sunset appeared—a desert phenomenon. Thirty miles on, we stopped at a hamlet called Newberry. I asked a man, idling on the porch of the store, about abandoned shacks.

"He said, 'Turn left a half mile down the road. Drive seven miles. Cross a dry river bed, turn right, and you'll see a two-room cabin. Move in.'

" 'Yours?' I asked.

" 'No. But that doesn't matter. Out here, anyone can move into any vacant cabin they come across. Just take care of things. Someday the owner may show up.'

" 'Water there?'

" 'A well and pump.'

"The man came to our car, looked in at Hulda, saw the baby in her lap, and said: 'The young one seems peaked. So was I when I came to the Mojave. Got well. Baby will, too.'

"I felt another strong surge of faith.

"The night grew dark, and as we drove along the smooth desert trail we marveled at the brilliance of the stars: millions of them, each seeming to hang from the sky on a thread of light. The cool, sharp air set the blood dancing in my veins.

"We turned right beyond the river bed, and the little cabin loomed suddenly in our headlights. I stopped close to it, rummaged in the back of the car, found the oil lamp, and filled it. I set it on the sand beside the cabin door. Moths flocked to it. Kangaroo rats hopped about, bewildered.

"I took the lamp inside the house and held it high. A double bed and a cot were in the front room, both without mattresses. In the other room was a table, a couple of chairs, and a wood range. That was about all.

"Back at the car, I took the baby from Hulda. As Hulda stepped out, she put her hand on my arm, looked up into the starry night and said: 'Thank You, God, for bringing us safely home.'

"I spread blankets on the beds, then began bringing in essential things from the car. Hulda and Tilde were both asleep in the double bed before I'd finished. I blew out the light, tiptoed to the cot, sat on its edge and took my shoes off. I heard the distant wail of a coyote. Next thing I knew, sunlight streamed through a cobwebbed window. Hulda and the baby were still asleep.

"I went to the kitchen, and three or four lizards scurried under a crumpled newspaper in a corner. I saw the house had been practically taken over by spiders. They were everywhere. While I was wondering if I could get rid of them before Hulda woke up, she spoke from behind me.

"'Go get wood for the fire, Ovid. But first, bring the broom from the car so I can clear the spiders out.'

"There was no wood, but I pulled roots of dead greasewood from the sand. They made a hot fire. I pumped brackish water from the well until it ran cool and clear. I realized that the river'd gone underground; the well tapped it.

"Back in the cabin, Hulda, a cloth wrapped around her head, hummed softly as she wielded the broom on ceiling, walls and floor. On my way to get more things from the car, I heard a noise like sand blowing gently against tin. A sidewinder rattlesnake coiled in the shade just back of a front tire.

"I'd already pictured little Tilde playing in the sandy yard, and I said: 'Dear God, protect our baby.' I hunted for a stick, didn't find one, and returned to the car. The snake was gone.

"That was three years ago. I've never seen a poisonous snake since within a quarter-mile of the cabin.

"Even after so long and sound a sleep, Tilde wakened as weak and listless as ever. Before the sun got too hot that morning, we followed Dr. Danskin's instructions, and let sunlight bathe Tilde's naked body for one minute. We did that for seven days, and when we saw there was no burning of her skin, we increased the sunbath to two minutes for the next seven days. By the end of that first month, Tilde was lying a full hour each day in direct sunlight. Her skin became a lovely golden-brown. She slept well, but lay inert, uncaring. She neither laughed nor cried. She looked at her dolls and toys as if she didn't see them.

"Twice that first month, I made trips to Barstow for fresh vegetables, mosquito netting, dishes, kerosene, staple foods, and other necessities. Then one afternoon I counted my money: twelve dollars and sixteen cents!

"Panic seized me. I stared into the hot distance. On the horizon all around, were mountains: the Calicos to my right, the White Mountains behind, the dark-red Newberry range to my left. To their feet stretched the flat sand, greasewood and cactus. Along the dry watercourse grew a few deep-rooted tamarisks and some yellowed willows. No human being, animal or bird was in sight.

"I walked. I followed a gravel-like ridge for miles, railing at myself, and at Dr. Danskin. Twelve dollars, and my family buried in this awful waste! I dared not leave them to go back to my job. I dared not stay—for where could I find work here! I laughed bitterly. Could God bring me an income out here among tarantulas, lizards, ants and scorpions?

"Twelve dollars would buy enough gas and oil to take us

to San Bernardino. We'd better leave at once—within an hour! I took a few fast steps toward home, and was brought up abruptly by a sidewinder coiled in my path. It was the first one I'd seen since that morning after our arrival.

"The snake itself was not evil, but it represented evil to me. I thought: *'A deadly snake has entered my garden of good thoughts. I'm in peril.'*

"In mental turmoil, I walked in a great circle until after the sun had set and the moon rose over the eastern hills. Stars winked out of an almost-purple sky. I sat on the sand, put my face in my hands, and said silently, 'Please, God, help me to think right again.'

"I thought: *It's there: the underground river—cool, pure and life-giving. All that's needed to make a paradise of this desert waste is for man to dig down and tap it. God's spirit is like that river. Through prayer, I dug a well of faith to His waters, but now I've let doubt choke up the well.*

"I urged my heart to reach beyond the stars. Gradually, peace came, and I felt one with the night, the wind and the heavens—one with the Spirit of God.

"When I entered our cabin, Hulda was sitting at the kitchen table. Lamplight made a halo of her hair. She looked at me with shining eyes, and said, 'This afternoon Tilde became interested in an ant on her bedside table. She watched it struggle with a bread crumb for several minutes. When it disappeared, she said: "Bring the ant back, Mama. I want to play with him." '

" 'An ant!'

" 'Yes. And when I promised it would come back tomorrow, she smiled, then dropped off to sleep. You'll have to make my promise good, Ovid.'

"I sat down and stared at Hulda. Ants! When I was a boy of ten, and had wearied of raising tadpoles in an old tub, my father had built for me what he called a formicary—a little narrow, earth-filled glass house. We'd put black ants in it, and I'd spent hours watching them.

"I said: 'If ants will arouse our little girl's interest in life, Hulda, ants she shall have.'

"I took the lamp and went out to look under the bedroom window. Sure enough, there was a harvester anthill. I got a board, slanted it from the top of the hill to the window. Inside, I pushed the small bedside table close to the sill, and scattered a bit of cereal on the table top. By daylight next morning, one line of ants was coming up the board and onto the table, while another line descended to the nest, carrying flakes of cereal.

"When Tilde wakened, I pointed to the ants, and moved her bed close to the table. Her eyes opened wide and she sat up and watched, intent but unsmiling. At last she looked up at Hulda and said, 'Tilde wants some just like ants want, Mama.'

"Tears filled Hulda's eyes as she prepared Tilde's breakfast. It was the first time our baby had *asked* for food in many a month.

"An inexpensive formicary can be built by making a frame and covering the sides with window glass held in place by adhesive tape. That's the type I'd intended to make. But at the lumber yard, I suddenly decided to build the very best formicary I could for my Tilde. That meant hardwood instead of pine, mitered corners, snug grooves for the glass. It meant buying a miter saw, a block plane, wood to make a miter box, sandpaper, wax for a wood finish, a narrow chisel, a narrow-sweep gouge, glue, and of course, glass.

"By the time I'd filled the car tank with gas, I'd spent twelve dollars and one cent. That left fifteen cents!

"Several times on the way home, I felt ill—as fear for the

future assailed me, yet I didn't regret my purchases. And I prayed the fears away.

"I built the formicary, and made a base from an old fir board that I planed, sandpapered and waxed. I rubbed and waxed the wooden frame, then stood back and admired my handiwork. It was a job to be proud of.

"Late that afternoon, Tilde and I went to the anthill, captured about seventy-five ants, dug up some eggs and larvae, and put them all through the little tin door. Almost immediately, the ants found an opening and began carrying the eggs and larvae through it down into the soil below. I dropped a moist wick through the door to act as a humidifier, and dropped in a small handful of oatmeal for food. I set the formicary by Tilde's bed.

"By the next morning the ants had built tunnels and rooms in the soil. Some were carrying food down through the notch; some were bringing up bits of food they could not utilize. By mid-afternoon, the ant colony was well established and thoroughly organized, and we could watch almost its every activity.

"Tilde's interest grew hour by hour. Not only did she watch, fascinated, but she began asking questions:

" 'Are those little white things really eggs? Are they filled with baby ants? Is it all right if my dollies watch the ants too?'

"It was a miracle. Almost overnight, our baby was her old, happy self. Our prayers were prayers of thanksgiving. Then another miracle followed.

"Three days after I'd placed the finished formicary in Tilde's room, a young entomology student from the University of Southern California stopped at our well to fill his canteen. He said he was spending a few days studying desert bees and other insects. I showed him the formicary. He was enthusiastic—said it was a lovely piece of work, and offered me fifteen dollars for it. I told him to come back the next day, and I'd have one just like it for him if he'd pay me ten dollars in advance, so I could buy materials. He smiled and handed me fifteen dollars.

"On the student's way home to Los Angeles, he stopped at the California Quarantine Station, at Daggett. One of the inspectors was also an entomology student. He saw the formicary, and the next evening drove out to our cabin and ordered one. A few days later I received a letter from the young student. He'd sold five formicaries to fellow students, and enclosed seventy-five dollars.

"Well, that's the way it went. One formicary sold another. Within six weeks, I was busy building formicaries from morning to night. And the pace continued for almost two years. I didn't make a big profit, but my income almost equaled what I'd have earned in the shipyard.

"And then, abruptly, the orders stopped coming. I said to Hulda: 'Tilde's as healthy as a colt. We've a nice little nest egg, because out here we've had few expenses. Seems to me the time's come to go somewhere else.'

"She answered: 'Yes, Ovid. And I've been thinking it's time that Tilde started to school. Let's pack things and be ready to go when God tells us where.'"

The bus pulled into the depot at San Bernardino. Damasch said, "I've an appointment here with a man from the Department of Agriculture. I've no idea why he sent for me, but he once bought one of my formicaries."

MORE THAN A year later, I got a letter from Damasch, from Germany. It said in part:

"So, because the Agricultural man I met at San Bernardino that day liked the workmanship of the formicary he'd bought from me, he recommended me for a job here in Ger-

many with a field section of the Agricultural Division of
the United Nations. Hulda is well. Tilde does well at school,
and is happy. We never cease to marvel at the way God directed us: the desert, the impulse to make a sturdy and beautiful formicary, everything. I look forward to advancement
here, for we are doing a great and good work. I know now,
that wherever men go—to desert or sea, mountain or plain,
or to strange, far lands—they will have happiness and security as long as they go with God."

SIR JAMES JEANS, noted English astronomer, once said that even so insignificant a thing as a baby throwing his rattle from his pram affects the farthest stars.

So, too, the prayers of even the most humble can affect the lives of millions.

Not far from Durban, Natal, is the town of Phoenix, and near Phoenix is a large house called Savodaya. The house was built by a friend of my father's—an Indian attorney who, dressed in the robes of a servant, fought long and prayerfully for civil rights for persecuted Indians. This attorney had a degree in law from a great English university. He was versed in philosophy, and his heart overflowed with love for the oppressed of the world. Because his skin was brown, he'd been thrown off South African trains, kicked by a policeman for walking on a sidewalk; had been imprisoned for peacefully protesting against discriminatory laws. One day while I was visiting Savodaya with my father, the attorney said:

"When discouraged, I sometimes go to Johannesburg to talk with Nath Gujarati. His prayerful faith in God inspires me to continue the 'good fight.' "

That's how I came to interview Gujarati. The result was "Dolls, Kittens and Puppies."

The name of the little attorney was Mohandas Karamchand Gandhi.

Dolls, Kittens, and Puppies

NATH GUJARATI SOLD dolls, kittens, and puppies in the Indian Bazaar at Vrededorp in Johannesburg. He was an East Indian, about fifty years old, a Christian, an Oxford graduate. He'd been a close friend of Mahatma Gandhi when Gandhi was a struggling, persecuted lawyer in South Africa. Although East Indians are anathema to many South Africans, Gujarati was loved by thousands on the Rand, and adored by children.

Gujarati was versed in law, medicine, music and literature. At Oxford he'd made intensive studies of religions of the world, and had become a Christian when he discovered that Jesus was the first great teacher who had preached love and understanding of children.

Gujarati's "store" was an awning-covered sidewalk stall in the bazaar. Dolls, made by him during business hours as he sat cross-legged on the ground, were displayed on a low table behind him. Live kittens were in a bright-red crate at his left; live puppies were in a yellow crate at his right. Tacked on the kittens' crate was a white pasteboard on which Gujarati'd written in beautiful large script this quotation from Southey: "A house is never perfectly furnished for enjoyment unless there is a child in it rising three years old, and a kitten rising three weeks."

One morning as I stood before Gujarati's booth waiting for a group of little boys to move on so I could talk to him,

a tall, stern-faced, gray-haired man paused before the sign on
the kitten crate. As he read, the man's face softened, then he
turned to look curiously at Gujarati. He gently pushed some
of the small boys aside, and gazed down thoughtfully at the
kittens. Finally he picked up a tiny rumpled, gray-and-black
creature with pale-blue eyes and a pointed, almost hairless
tail.

"How much?" he asked.

Gujarati said: "A penny if you're poor. A pound if you're
rich."

"I'm not rich," the man said, "but I've a grandson exactly
three years old."

"You love a child," Gujarati said, "therefore, you are
rich."

The man seemed startled. "So I am," he said wonderingly,
"so I am." He placed a golden sovereign in Gujarati's palm,
tucked the kitten inside his coat and hurried away, the kitten's head sticking out above a button.

Gujarati then turned to a little boy who, with one rumpled
stocking down around his ankle, sat with face pressed
against the puppy crate. In Dutch, Gujarati said, "I've sold
a kitten for a pound, Wilhelm, so you may have your puppy
for a penny."

One of the small boy's hands reached into his pants pocket
for a coin. At the same time, with the other hand, the boy
lifted the puppy by the scruff of the neck. The puppy yelped.
The penny fell to the ground as Wilhelm used both hands
to cuddle the wriggling, black puppy against his face.

Gujarati smiled as I picked up the penny and handed it
to him. The group of boys crowded around Wilhelm, each
trying to pet the puppy. Wilhelm, sniffling with joy, held the
boys off as best he could. It was then that I noticed the sign
on the puppy crate: "Blessed is the man who gives pleasure
to a child."

"Mr. Gujarati," I said, "I want to write a story about you. I understand that with your background, you could have been a successful lawyer, or doctor, or possibly a great musician. Yet you chose to sell toys and pets for children. Why?"

Before he could answer, an anxious-faced woman stopped at the booth, holding the hand of a small girl. She said:

"We bought a dolly here some time ago. Betty loved it. It's lost, and nothing will do but another dolly like it. We've bought several wonderfully realistic dolls, but Betty puts them carefully to bed, and leaves them there. She named your doll Pearl, and we don't know why—for it was scraggly . . ."

"Children admire beautiful, hard-bodied, modern dolls, Madam," Gujarati said, "but soft, snuggly dolls are the ones they *love*. They can hold them closer to their hearts."

"Of course," the mother said. "Soft—like babies." She knelt, and with an arm around her little girl, pointed wordlessly to the dolls on the table. Betty reached for one, and Gujarati handed it to her. Then he watched quietly as the doll was clasped tightly in the small arms that had been too long empty.

The mother opened her purse. "Still a penny for the poor, and a pound for the rich?" she asked with a smile. She put a sovereign on the table, then a second one beside it. "The extra pound will buy a dolly for someone who hasn't a penny," she said.

Gujarati said: "Madam, your gift has brought you closer to heaven."

After the mother and child had gone, Gujarati wrapped up a doll, called a ricksha boy, and gave delivery instructions in Zulu. To me, he then said: "There are so many, many children who haven't the penny." He sat down with crossed legs and began to sew. I stood watching him, waiting.

"It is true," he said at last, "that I might have made a

success in other works, but I chose to work with children because they are like what Jesus would have us be.

"As a young student, I yearned for a depictment of the true
God. I studied the philosophies of the Orient, of Greece, of
Rome, of Egypt, and of modern Europe. Philosophers had
piled complication upon complication. Nowhere did I find a
concept of God that my soul could understand or accept. The
result was that I came close to atheism."

Gujarati looked up at me intently. "Do you know," he
asked, "that unselfish yearning of the spirit is prayer?"

"Yes, I know," I said.

"And do you know that God always answers when we pray
truly?"

"Yes," I said.

"Well," Gujarati said, "God led me to read the words of
Jesus: the Sermon on the Mount, the Lord's Prayer, and His
words about children: 'Suffer the little children to come unto me; forbid them not: for to such belongeth the kingdom
of God. Verily I say unto you, Whosoever shall not receive
the kingdom of God as a little child, he shall in no wise enter
therein.'

"I state sadly that many Occidentals read Jesus' words
without realization of the truths contained in them. To an
Oriental like myself, Jesus' words have great impact. The
key to eternal God is in His words—the key to all that is good.

"Well, my soul's search had ended. I would become as a
little child in Jesus' arms. In my new-found joy, I memorized
all of Jesus' own words. I then asked God how I could best
use my special talents and capacities to serve him. The answer
was unmistakable: 'Inasmuch as ye have done it unto one of
these, my little ones, ye have done it unto Me.'

"Here on the edge of Johannesburg's slums, I started this
business. Here I could help to bring happiness to under-
privileged little ones. I chose to sell kittens, puppies, and

dolls, for to be loved and to have something to love, is the need of all children."

As Gujarati talked, he was interrupted from time to time by customers—old men and women, young men and women, mothers with children, fathers with children, parents alone, and children alone. Some arrived sad-eyed and worried. All left with new brightness in their faces. And Gujarati seemed always to know exactly the right things to say.

An impatient, harried Dutch woman sternly hushed a two-year-old girl as the youngster squealed in delight at the kittens. Gujarati said: "How sad you would be if you were never to hear your little girl's voice again."

The woman's face paled, and she looked at Gujarati for a moment with horrified eyes, then said: "Yes. Oh, thank you—thank you. I'll always remember."

We were interrupted by several boys who knelt and began to bark back in glee at the barking puppies. A passing policeman said harshly: "You boys try to act like men, or go on home."

Gujarati glanced up at the officer. "Is the world, then, all grown up?" he asked.

The policeman laughed. "Bark away, lads," he said to the boys, and walked on.

Gujarati watched the officer move on down the street. Then he said to me: "Policemen are sometimes impatient with us Indians. That officer wasn't really scolding the boys; he was indirectly scolding me."

"Your business seems successful," I said.

"Financially?"

"Yes."

"It is, but making money is not all of business. As surely as I know that I live, I know that a business which follows the path of goodness will not only bring money to its owner, but will bring delight to all who do business with that owner. In business, a man must accept God's direction as a child accepts that of his father. If the man will do that, he will prosper, and his soul will be at peace."

"Will you put the rewards of this business—God's business—into words for me, Mr. Gujarati?" I asked. "I'd like to use your words as the ending of my article."

Gujarati's reply was postponed while two Europeans stopped to look at the puppies. One nudged the other and pointed to the sign. "Puppies are an awful nuisance about the house," he said.

His companion replied, "When I was a kid, I had a black-and-tan mutt named Joe. He slept with me, fleas and all. I was ten when he died. My mother said Joe'd gone to dog heaven. I cried for hours because they wouldn't let me go to dog heaven too."

The first man said: "I guess I've been wrong not to let Frankie have a dog. Which one of these would you choose for an eight-year-old?"

For twenty minutes the two men prodded, picked up, felt, and scrutinized puppies. They pulled ears, looked into mouths, examined teeth. They chuckled and laughed, having the time of their lives. And they might have stayed all the rest of the day, had Gujarati not said:

"Dogs and boys have two things in common—loyalty and a capacity for love. Choose any pup; your boy will love it, and the pup will love him. Choose even the ugliest; it will not matter, for to a boy, all dogs are beautiful."

So the beaming father picked out a puppy. As the two men left, the second man turned to Gujarati and winked.

"Three will now be happy," Gujarati said to me, "a boy, a father, and a friend." He went back to his work on the dolls, and as the needle flicked in and out, he said, "My reward is in my soul. Perhaps I can best tell it in a slight paraphrase of Alexander Maclaren's words:

" 'In my heart now is the quiet of the green, inland valleys of our Father's land, where no tempest comes any more,
nor the loud winds are ever heard; all mystery gone, and all
rebellion hushed and silenced, and all unrest at an end forever.' "

T'OWARD the close of her career, Margaret Madden, the schoolteacher who learned to pray, was asked to state briefly the gist of what she'd learned about children during her years of teaching. She replied:

"I learned that when spiritual need is satisfied, all physical drives assume their normal functions in the scheme of life."

Miss Madden made that statement many years before Dr. Viktor Frankl, president of the Austria Society of Medical Psychotherapy, shook the foundations of psychiatry by announcing that the powerful urge to find God is the dominating force of our lives.

A large section of America's population lives in fear. This fear, according to surveys, is of financial, domestic, physical and spiritual insecurity—not, as we've been led to suppose, fear of falling bombs or enemy infiltration.

"When one finds God," Miss Madden said, "all fear is dispelled; and finding God is entirely a matter of prayer— a simple request that God, who Himself has said that He is within you, reveal Himself to you."

The Teacher Who Learned to Pray

IN 1919 WHEN Margaret Madden, newly graduated from teachers' college, arrived in a small California cow town, she saw streets ankle-deep in dust, broken wooden sidewalks, unpainted houses, and shabby stores with ugly false fronts. The few trees along the main street were dejected. The church on the corner wore an air of discouragement.

Yet a few months later, that little town began to take on charm. Within eight years, streets were tree-lined, homes were painted, lawns were neat. Sidewalks were wide and well-laid. The church had been faced with brick. All false store-fronts had been replaced with honest, modern façades.

Where many children had once graduated from high school only to leave for cities as quickly as possible, most graduates now stayed, or returned to grow and prosper.

There are other towns in California as tidy and charming as this one, but unlike others, this town admits that it owes its present enviable condition to prayer; chiefly to the prayers of a little girl named Myrtle, and of one woman, Margaret Madden.

"That morning thirty-two years ago," Miss Madden told me when I interviewed her, "my heart sang as the bus took me through the countryside toward the scene of my new duties. I was about to begin realizing dreams I'd held through college years. I pictured the little town I'd never seen as a quiet, green village of happy homes and laughing children. I was eager to arrive and to begin teaching.

"As the bus pulled into the main street, my heart sank. I'd never imagined any place so dreary. As I stepped to the ground, the churning wheels of the departing bus covered me with fine, red dust. I crossed the street, dust spurting with each step like little bomb explosions. By the time I reached the sidewalk, my best suit, blouse, hat, gloves, shoes, stockings and purse, were a mess.

"No one had met me. A few overall-clad men stared unsmiling as I walked down the block past store-windows filled with sun-faded merchandise. I turned a corner and saw my school. Its yellow paint was peeling. Steps that led to the narrow porch were splintery and askew. The playground was sandy waste, dotted with weeds.

"Dislike of the town was suddenly so intense that I felt nauseated. I sat on the school steps and struggled to regain normal perspective.

"An approaching man paused when he saw me, then came and stood before me.

" 'You the new teacher?' he asked.

" 'Yes,' I said.

" 'Well, you look awful young. I hope you've no hifalutin' ideas about education. What we want in this town is reading, writing and arithmetic. You understand what I mean?'

"I couldn't answer.

"He said: 'I'm Meyer—the School Board.'

"I nodded, and watched him stride away. I sat a long time, and the longer I sat, the greater became my urge to go away on the next bus. As I got to my feet, I heard the back of my skirt tear—caught by a large splinter. I quickly located the boardinghouse, explained I was ill, and was shown to my room. Feeling trapped, and forlorn, I lay on the bed and cried.

"Next morning I still felt I couldn't go through with it.

I pictured long, dismal months ahead in this town of dead hopes. As I walked to the school, however, I tried to see things from a realistic viewpoint. After a few months—perhaps a year—I could get a transfer. As I entered the school, I felt better.

"I'd intended greeting my twenty-three new eighth-grade pupils with a cheerful 'good-morning,' but as I faced them, my heart sank to a new low. They were in keeping with the rest of the town—unkempt, all—dressed in patched and faded dresses and jeans. It was evident, too, that some had come directly to school from the barnyard.

"At last I spoke, and my voice was so edged that it grated even on me. The room grew tense. There was resentment and dislike in the eyes that stared at me. I looked from face to face. Some were impassive. Some were sullen. Only one little face was friendly—that of a blue-eyed girl named Myrtle.

"The second month was increasingly unhappy. The children developed a passive resistance. None actually rebelled, but they often failed to do homework. Tardiness increased. Recitations were poor. The class seemed unnaturally quiet, and I grew more nervous, knowing that coldly appraising eyes were always on me. I forced myself to be kindly, but the children sensed my true feelings. I tried being strict. They grew more unresponsive.

"I began to fear for my job. I imagined the principal looked at me with doubt. I developed what I thought was a heart condition. My heart would begin a heavy, rapid beating that caused a feeling of panic. Then the pounding would end abruptly, and my heart would slow until I feared it would stop altogether.

"By the end of that month, sleep had become impossible without pills. Each night I'd waken several times with a terrifying sense of impending loss. I feared constantly, but what, I didn't know.

"One morning Myrtle Anderson was the only pupil to turn in homework. All others made excuses. This was open rebellion, and I lost control of myself. Coldly, in detail, I told the children what I thought of them and of the town they lived in. Then my heart began its terrible racing, and I collapsed. Myrtle ran for the principal. He sent for the doctor, and dismissed my class for the day.

"Doctor O'Brien said, 'Your heart's all right, Miss Madden. Your trouble's nerves.' He looked stern, and added, 'You need to find some interests in life aside from yourself, young lady. If you can't find them—try praying.' He picked up his bag and told me to go home and to bed. 'I'll stop by and see you tomorrow,' he said. Dennis, his grandson, was one of my pupils.

"That afternoon as I lay dozing in my room, Myrtle's grandmother, a little bird-like, eighty-year-old lady, came to visit. She brought a bouquet of sweet-william, and a red-letter Testament.

"She said, 'Myrtle has told me a great deal about you, Miss Madden. She remembers you in her prayers every night. I've marked some passages in this Testament. Read them, and think about them. You're a fine young woman, and God needs you to do great things in this town of ours.'

" 'Mrs. Anderson,' I said, 'I wouldn't stay in this town for twice the amount of money I earn.'

" 'It's a sad little town,' she said. 'The war took so many of our boys and girls. Some came back, but they wouldn't stay. We've lost almost a whole generation. The children you're teaching now are our hope for the future. You can help them so much . . . you can inspire this whole town . . .'

"She patted my hand, smiled, and left me. I lay a long

time, thinking. I'd never thought of the town as having
lost its youth because of the war. I'd never thought of the
residents as hoping that the present generation—my class—
would be able to take over and carry on some day.

"I fingered the red-letter Testament curiously. I'd never
really read a Bible. I knew little of religion. My parents
had seldom mentioned it. As for prayer—that was something
for the superstitious. Self-sufficiency had been my credo . . .
prayer was not for me.

"Inwardly, I smiled at the suggestions of prayer that had
come from old Doctor O'Brien, and now from this little old
lady. But as I thought of Myrtle kneeling each night, asking
God to help me, tears came to my eyes. I fell asleep with the
Testatment in my hand.

"Next morning I wakened with an odd sense of anticipa-
tion—and with the astonishing realization that I'd slept
soundly all night without pills. I lay a while, wondering—
wishing I were the type who could sincerely believe in so
simple a thing as prayer. And all this while, my hand lay
on the Testament. I opened it, and glanced at a red-printed
paragraph. It was Matthew 4:4. Remember, I'd never before
opened a Bible except in skepticism.

"I read: *It is written, Man shall not live by bread alone,
but by every word that proceedeth out of the mouth of God.*'

"With a wonderful sense of discovery, I read on and on.
I read the Sermon on the Mount, and wept because of its
beauty. I came to a paragraph that Myrtle's grandmother
had marked:

" *. . . your Father knoweth what things ye have need of
before ye ask Him.*'

"I turned the pages, and came to another marked paragraph:

" *Ask and it shall be given you; seek, and ye shall find;
knock, and it shall be opened unto you.*'

"I thumbed the Testament page by page, reading each marked verse. Light began to dawn in my mind. Bless the little old lady. With a wavering pencil, she'd pointed out reasons for my failure, and had shown me the way to success. She'd double-marked this verse: *'Take heed that ye despise not one of these little ones . . .'*

"And this: *'Feed my lambs . . .'*

"I won't go into all the hours I spent becoming aware, and aghast, at my selfishness. I wondered how I'd grown so self-centered. I finally admitted to myself that it'd been because I'd tried to live without God. I remember saying softly, something like this:

" 'God, forgive me, and help me to gain the love and respect of my pupils so I can teach them the good way of life.'

"It was an unselfish prayer, and my heart was truly contrite. And from that moment, I've had no heart condition. I've had no panic. I've felt secure in the love of Jesus, and I've worked with His guidance."

Miss Madden sat back in the chair as if our interview were over.

I said, "Please don't stop there, Miss Madden. Tell the rest of your story."

She looked at me gravely.

"I'll always feel humble when I think of what followed," she said. "Before school commenced next morning, I went to the principal's office and told him of my experience . . . about learning to pray . . . about the discovery of my selfishness. I told him that above all else, I now wanted to stay on here, and to devote my life to the children and to the town. He smiled, reached for a folded paper on his desk, tore it into strips and dropped the strips in the wastebasket. Later, I learned that that paper had been my discharge.

"It was difficult to face the children that morning. I prayed silently as I stood before them, not knowing what to say. Words came—the right ones. I said:

" 'You boys and girls are the future adults of this little town. In this room now, I believe, is a future mayor, future members of the town councils, future businessmen and women, and future school teachers. We must work together, you and I, to make our town a better place in which to live. You girls and boys are the ones who best know what improvements you'd like; and you are the ones to make them. There are so many things that . . .'

"A black-haired boy, George Meyer, son of the head of the School Board, held up his hand and waved so eagerly that I stopped speaking and nodded to him.

"He said, 'What this town needs, Miss Madden, is prettier houses. My own house is the ugliest of all.'

"He'd barely finished speaking when Hans Mueller, a thin, sensitive lad, said, 'Paint. Beautiful colors on the buildings. Bright paint. I'd like to paint every house. I'd . . .' Suddenly shy, Hans sat back, blushing.

"Suggestions came rapidly. Better business buildings, sidewalks, paved streets, green lawns, trees, shrubs and flowers, a modern school building. A fat lad, Larry Rogers, stood and said defiantly:

" 'Plumbing is what this town needs.' Everyone laughed. Larry's father was a plumber.

"That's how it all began. Within a week, we'd worked out the start of a project. George, who surprised me with his ability as an artist, made a drawing of his home on a large sheet of butcher paper. The house was a big, two-story box with windows spaced mathematically on all sides. No trees, no shrubs—just ugly straight lines. On another sheet of paper, George drew the house as he'd like it—a wide front porch, a low shallow-roofed wing on one side, a trellised portico on the other.

"With crayons, Hans colored the improved house plan as he'd like it painted. I was delighted, for Hans had a true sense of color harmony. We needed trees, shrubs and grass to complete the picture, and the whole class suggested where plantings should go. Finally we had a drawing in color that showed a sweeping drive, tall shrubs breaking straight corner lines of the building, vines growing over the portico, a lawn, a cement sidewalk at the street, and flowers everywhere. Hans was like a boy transformed as he colored in the class's suggestions. George's face shone.

"That evening, George's father stomped into my room, after a heavy knock on the door. He scowled as he asked, 'What've you done to my boy?'

"Before I could speak, his face softened, and he said: 'George came home from school tonight with gleaming eyes. He showed me the drawing your class made of our house. Miss Madden, to see my son eager and interested means more to me than . . . than . . .' He blew his nose loudly. 'I tell you, Teacher, that house plan is a masterpiece. Those kids are good. I'm going to hire carpenters, and follow the plan exactly as it's drawn. If the kids want to come and work after school and on Saturdays, I'll pay them wages.' He took a deep breath and added: 'My mind's made up!'

"There was a lump in my throat as I thanked him. He shook my hand vigorously, and as he walked down the hall, I heard him blowing his nose like a bugle.

"George's mother joined the project too, and asked my class to help rearrange the kitchen, design and make drapes, choose new rugs, and other furnishings.

"Months later, the remodeled home, shining with new paint and enhanced by trees, grass and flowers, became the county's showplace. People came miles to look at it. Other residents began asking the class to re-design or make suggestions for improvement of their homes and buildings. That initial project, like the Olympic Torch, has been passed from that first class, to each of my succeeding ones.

"And various phases of The Project required that my classes study fascinating by-way subjects. For instance, reading about shingles took us to cedar forests, and that in turn led us to deforestation, and then to reforestation. Cement led us to lime. Lime led to kilns and to rock formations. In working out plans for lawns, we got into types of soils, land management, and food production. Before we were through with our first house—the Meyer home—we'd ranged briefly, but eagerly, through many fields of knowledge.

"George Meyer—now in his forties—is a partner in this area's largest contracting firm. Hans Mueller and his wife—she was also a former pupil of mine—are now successful commercial artists. Larry Rogers owns a hardware store—and does the town plumbing. Another boy, Otis Hardinge, who joined The Project later, is our town's leading banker. Young Dennis O'Brien is now Dr. O'Brien."

Dr. Clark Robinson, San Francisco educator, and author of *Making the Most of School and Life* (Macmillan), said recently:

"Prayer enabled Miss Madden to innovate her Project thirty years before that method of teaching was accepted as the latest concept in education. She discovered children's aptitudes, and put them to work on matters affecting *everyday life*. Miss Madden taught her pupils also the importance of each person in the Scheme of Things. We need teachers who pray."

T O BETTER overcome the evils of a world in turmoil, the 83rd Congress recently opened a small room in the Capitol, where, as Speaker Sam Rayburn said, members can be alone with their God. The room, which is for Representatives and Senators only, is dedicated to meditation and prayer.

The establishment of this Prayer Room has done much to revive the faith of Americans who are thus reminded that according to our Declaration of Independence, our legislators are elected "to secure to the People those inalienable Rights with which we have been endowed by our Creator."

Today, if you ask almost any man you meet, he will tell you that he is convinced that World Peace must have a Spiritual source. That is why more and more voters are asking God's guidance when they go to the polls. And that is why today we have a Congress of praying men—475 of them, according to a recent survey.

Here I tell the prayer story of Governor Goodwin Knight, of California. I could tell similar stories about many other legislative leaders, but I tell Knight's because I know it best.

Public Servant of God

WHEN GOODWIN KNIGHT, California's Governor, was twelve years old, he was told that the family fortune had been lost in the mining business; that he was now a poor boy and would likely have to make his own way in life. Young Knight thought about his problem and finally decided that it was too big for a boy to solve by himself. That night he asked God to help him choose a career, and to direct him in making that career a success.

From that day, Knight has been successful in his every major undertaking. Although he gained greatest renown as a lawyer, superior-court judge, lieutenant governor, and governor, Knight is primarily a businessman. Because he follows God's guidance in every transaction, he has known no failures.

"God wants us to make money," Knight says, "but I believe that in order to be truly successful, a man must achieve —in addition to money—honor, dignity, and the love of those who know him.

"There is a sureness, a *quietness* that results from prayer. When a man knows in his heart that he is proceeding as God directs, his dealings are conducted with a deep sense of harmony and peace.

"Prayer makes available the power of God. Prayer has an awesome force, for it is always answered. We cannot tell how nor when that answer will come, but come it will, if we keep in tune with divine harmonies.

"As I look back on my life, I see that every move I made,

every job I took, was part of God's plan for me—the plan for which I asked Him when I was a worried and fearful boy. It makes me appreciative and humble.

"At the time I asked God to direct my career, I also prayed that He would help me recover the money my father had lost. That prayer, too, was answered—many years later.

"When I was thirteen I developed an urge to write a book. I had no illusions about being a writer. I knew perfectly well that a book by a boy of thirteen would earn very little money. Yet the urge grew until I could no longer resist it. I wrote a book for boys. It was published and actually made a little money.

"After I became mature I realized that God had directed me to write that story of adventure in which honesty and decency won out over selfishness and evil, so that through the long hours of composition I would develop and solidify the character pattern on which my future was to be based."

To earn money for college, Knight worked in a grocery store during vacations—twelve hours a day for nine dollars a week. Knight says:

"I attended Manual Arts High School in Los Angeles, where I saw the prayers of a godly principal imbue a class of students with pride and confidence in the good within their fellow men. That was the class of 1915, known as the 'wonder class' because so many of its members attained high and honorable places in adult life."

Before entering Stanford University, Knight worked for a year as a mucker in a mine. At Stanford he waited tables to help pay expenses. His intention was to become a mining engineer like his father, but he switched to the study of law. He became manager of the Stanford yearbook, took a postgraduate course at Cornell University, and began a private law practice in Los Angeles.

His legal practice became prosperous. Then. while vacationing in the Mojave Desert, he got into conversation with an old prospector, who said:

"Name's Knight, huh? Thirty years ago I knew a man named Jesse Knight. We located some gold claims together, and he went off to raise money so we could work them. He never came back."

"Jesse Knight was my father," Knight said. "What happened to the gold claims?"

"Never been touched."

Knight said: "Let's go and look at them."

When Knight saw the claims, he *knew* that here was the answer to his prayer of long ago; that God would help him retrieve the fortune his father had lost. He went back to Los Angeles, closed out his legal business, invested the money in tools and equipment, and began mining. He named the claims the *Elephant* and the *Eagle*.

Knight avoided labor troubles by making every employee a shareholder. He conducted the business with the confidence that comes from daily prayer. To the amazement of almost everyone but himself, the *Elephant* and *Eagle* became two of the best-paying mining properties in the Southwest. He eventually sold out for far more than his father had lost years before.

Now in possession of a comfortable fortune, Knight decided he could serve Los Angeles and its citizens best by becoming a superior-court judge. His character and ability were recognized by the governor of California, and the appointment was made. Two years later, he was elected for the full six-year term. In the campaign, he avoided the usual charges and countercharges of petty politics.

As a judge, Knight prayed before making each decision. The fame of his wisdom and understanding spread. He became a candidate for lieutenant-governor. Asking God to direct his efforts, he campaigned quietly, and was swept into office by the largest vote ever accorded a candidate for that office. In 1950, he was re-elected on both the Democratic and Republican tickets. He did very little campaigning, but the voters of California gave Lieutenant-Governor Knight 3,089,278 votes—the largest vote ever received by a candidate for public office in the history of the United States, excepting candidates for President, or Vice-President.

Knight points out that as a grocery clerk in a poverty-ridden section of Los Angeles, he developed sympathy and understanding for the poor. As a mucker in a mine, he learned the problems of men who toil with their hands. As a waiter, he learned courtesy and the joy of service. As manager of the Stanford yearbook, and as the owner of a mine, he learned efficiency in business. As a lawyer and a judge, he saw all facets of human nature. And above all, he learned that God is a never-failing source of help and strength in all circumstances.

Knight hesitated about entering State politics. California was experiencing some unhealthy pressure from the politically powerful, particularly from a clique controlled by a liquor lobbyist.

"But," says Knight, "I have long maintained that praying men and women must take active interest in civic and political affairs if this nation is to survive. They must assume public duties, no matter how unpleasant some of those duties may seem. They must bring prayer to government. I could not do less than I advocated for others.

"There are those who hold the belief that prayer is vain and old-fashioned. Some of these unfortunates are in power in this country, but they are a small minority. The majority of Americans are loyal to God. We are a great nation. To continue as a great nation, we need God's guiding hand— and prayer is the open door to that guidance."

Abraham Lincoln, who piloted America through her

stormiest seas, was a praying man too. In speaking of some of the Union's darkest hours, he said:

"I have been driven many times to my knees, by the overwhelming conviction that I had nowhere else to go. My own wisdom, and that of all about me, seemed insufficient for the day."

The value of praying schoolteachers in forming the minds and characters of future governmental, civic, and business leaders cannot be overestimated. I know stories of many teachers whose prayers have helped bring beauty and prosperity to their communities.

In 1915, Los Angeles Manual Arts High School graduated one of the most outstanding classes in American high school history. It was a new school then; its students chiefly from workers' homes. Pupils of more *élite* schools referred to Manual Arts students as roughnecks. In those days, as today, teachers and principals were underpaid, pestered by politicians, their private lives spied upon by community busybodies. Obstacles confronting Manual Arts High School in 1915 were more difficult to surmount than those faced by high schools of today. Forty-eight-year-old Principal Albert Wilson needed help for his program. He got it from God.

Wilson believed, as did Thomas Grey, that the different degrees of education may be compared to the artificer's operations upon marble:—it is one thing to dig it out of the quarry, and another to square it, to give it gloss and lustre, call forth every beautiful spot and vein, shape it into a column, or animate it into a statue. Wilson's constant prayer was that God would help him bring forth "every beautiful spot and vein" in the marble he had been given to work.

He didn't pray for the discomfiture of the politicians. He didn't pray for a change of heart on the part of local gossips. He didn't pray for increased salary. Yet, those things came to pass.

He didn't tell God how he wanted to run the school. He asked only that he be permitted to operate under God's direction. Then he and his teachers went to work. The graduates? Here are the names of some of them:

Frank Capra, and Tay Garnett, internationally noted motion picture directors; Erskine Johnson, and Jose Rodriquez, of writing, newspaper and radio fame; Rob Wagner, publisher of *Script*, once known as the one-man Humane Society of Hollywood because he forced the movie industry to stop cruelty to animal actors; Buron Fitts, one-time Lieutenant Governor of California, World War I hero, and Los Angeles District Attorney; Clark Teitsworth, vice-president of Socony Vacuum Oil Company; General Jimmy Doolittle; Major General Paul Williams; Brigadier General Harold Harris; Appellate Court Judge Marshall McComb; Judges Louis Kauffman, Joseph Marchetti, Jesse Frampton; Marion Morgan, internationally-known dancing and gymnastics teacher; Phyllis Haver and Helen Jerome Eddy, motion picture actresses; Maud Howell, George Arliss' dramatic coach; Lawrence Tibbett, opera singer; Goodwin Knight, Governor of California; and many others now active in national, state and local affairs.

That was the class of 1915. Since then, year after year, Manual Arts has graduated classes whose members have become constructive, *praying* leaders in all walks of life.

Teachers who pray, parents who pray, officials who pray, children who pray. That is America—God's America. And lest we forget that it *is* God's America, President Eisenhower recently added two words to our Pledge to the Flag. Here is that pledge with those two words underlined:

I pledge allegiance to the flag of the United States of America, and to the Republic for which it stands, one nation, *under God,* indivisible, with liberty and justice for all.

And it might be well to repeat here that the root word for God, the Aryan *gheu,* means—*to pray.*

MORE than thirty years after the incidents in this prayer story, I met Joe Houghton in South Africa. He'd just completed building a difficult section of telegraph line in Ethiopia, using tall steel poles—tall, to prevent giraffes breaking the wires with their long necks—steel, because termites consumed wooden poles in a night. As in the "Christmas Lights" story, Houghton owed his Ethiopian success to prayer. He said:

"I pray, then wrestle."

"Wrestle?"

"Like Stanislaus Zabysco, the time he was sentenced to be shot by the Russians."

I didn't know, so Houghton went on:

"Zabysco was a Polish physician, who became world's champion wrestler. During World War I he was captured by Russian soldiers, and sentenced to death. Thinking to have fun with him, the Russians offered to free him if he could defeat their wrestling champion. In telling me about it, Zabysco said, 'So I prayed that God would give me strength and good judgment. Then I dug in and wrestled—and won.'"

Christmas Lights

ONE BITTER ARCTIC winter about thirty years ago, Fairbanks-Morse Company of Canada took a contract to install a light-and-power plant in the Far-North town of Fort Pelly, Saskatchewan—a cluster of about seventy houses huddled about the MacKenzie trading post. The small powerhouse had been built, engines and generators installed, and houses wired; but when Fairbanks-Morse tried to get a contractor to build the power line, firm after firm turned down the job as too difficult in weather that might include temperatures lower than fifty degrees below zero.

Residents had almost resigned themselves to oil lamps, lanterns and candles for another long winter, when Mayor Grey, of Winnipeg, one of Canada's top engineers, told Fairbanks-Morse officials:

"There are two young fellows, Paul Klein and Johnny Habine, who own a contracting outfit up near Saskatoon. Why don't you contact them?"

Klein and Habine took the contract. They put Joe Houghton, a recent graduate from the Canadian Veterans' Rehabilitation Electrical Course, in charge of the job.

"Joe," Habine said, "we're laying this job in your lap because you haven't had enough experience to realize how difficult it's going to be. It's a small job, but a mean one. We can make money on it if you finish it by Christmas. And remember: *Nothing's impossible with God's help.*"

"Okay," Joe said.

So Houghton and two helpers, Allan Norman and Dan Borton, each driving a horse-drawn bobsled heavily laden with line-building materials, arrived at Fort Pelly in late October. For a week, winds hissed down from the Porcupine Mountains. Snow, soft and feathery when falling gently, became flakes of ice that bit into faces like particles of fire. The nearby Swan River froze deep. Communications with the outside world ceased. Fort Pelly crouched, snowed-in.

When the winds died, Houghton snowshoed three miles to an Indian village to hire labor. The Indians said: "Too cold to work now. Come back in the spring."

Poles, wires, crossarms, insulators and guy wires had been unloaded and piled behind the blacksmith shop. While Joe laid out the two miles of line, Norman and Borton used horses to drag poles through the drifts to their locations. They drilled the poles for crossarms, bolted on the braces, screwed on insulators. They made a wire reel from a wagon wheel, and with a horse hitched to one end of the coils of heavy No. 00 weatherproof wire, stretched it out along the snow, ready to be lifted to the crossarms when the poles were erected.

Temperatures remained at fifty-five degrees below zero. The sun rose about ten o'clock each morning, and night fell in the middle of each afternoon. Much of the work went on in darkness.

Work hours were long. The men took turns going to the post store to warm their feet, which were often near to frostbite despite heavy socks and two pairs of moccasins. Much work was accomplished. Houghton believed they'd be able to turn power into the line by Christmas.

But the townsfolk were not optimistic. They told Houghton and his men that no sourdough would even think of trying to dig holes in ground frozen rock-hard six feet or more deep. "Give it up until spring," they advised. "You're making fools of yourselves."

Houghton knew his problem was tough. A day or two earlier, he'd cleared away ice and snow to bare a patch of ground, and had swung a sharp-pointed pick with all of his strength. A frozen chip of earth had flown up and cut his cheek, but the pick point had not penetrated the ground so much as an inch. He'd said to Norman:

"Seventy-five holes to dig. How're we going to do it?"

"It can't be done, Joe," Norman had said. "To dig one four-foot hole in ground like this would take a man ten days. Seventy-five of them . . . We'll just have to wait for the thaw."

In his icy bedroom later, Joe prayed: "I'm going to sleep tonight, God, with my mind open to You. I believe I'll have the answer when I waken."

To Pete Petrie, the blacksmith, Joe said next morning:

"Steel rods, an inch in diameter, heated red-hot, will penetrate frozen ground, Pete."

"Yes," Petrie said, "but only about half an inch before they cool off."

"If we drive them with sledge hammers, how far?"

"Maybe an inch."

"We'd have to heat the rod forty-eight times to get it down four feet," Houghton said.

"Look," Petrie said kindly. "Everybody in town is for you, but you're not going to be able to dig those holes in time to get lights this Christmas. Wait for spring. You'll be just as far ahead. Anyway, suppose you *do* sink a hole with a rod. Then what?"

"Dynamite," Joe said.

Petrie laughed. "Did you ever try to dynamite frozen ground?"

"No."

"Come on, I'll show you." They went out behind the shop and cleared away some snow. Petrie heated a pointed inch rod white-hot, handed Houghton a sixteen-pound sledge, and they ran to the cleared spot. Petrie pressed the sizzling rod against the ground and said, "Hit it hard, boy. Hit it hard."

Houghton swung six times, and each time felt the rod sink a little. The seventh time there was no downward movement. The rod had cooled. The hole was one inch deep.

Thirty-six times, Petrie ran from forge to hole with the glowing, pointed rod. Thirty-six times Houghton pounded it repeatedly with the sledge. When the rod had been driven down three feet, Petrie brought a stick of dynamite he'd been thawing in a kettle of hot water. He pressed in the fused cartridge, pushed the charge down into the hole, tamped it hard with snow, lit the fuse and moved back.

From a safe distance, they watched the explosion lift great chunks of frozen earth into the air a few feet. Where the chunks *had* been was now a crater four feet deep and six feet wide.

"You see?" Petrie said.

"Yes, I see. But we'll go ahead anyway. You make two small forges, Pete, that we can set up near pole locations. Borton and Norman'll punch half the holes. I'll hire some fellow, and he and I'll punch the other half."

"You're crazy," Petrie said. "How're you going to fill the craters after you set the poles? Ground, sandpiles—everything around here's frozen solid."

"I'll find a way," Houghton said.

So seventy-five fantastic holes were blown—and the residents of Fort Pelly laughed. Houghton had to admit that blasting out a cubic yard or two of frozen earth, in order to set a lightweight cedar pole, seemed ridiculous. And there seemed no way to fill those yawning cavities. He'd tried his pick in a snow-covered pile of sand. It was a solid block. He'd tried breaking the chunks blasted from the holes, and found it'd take longer to break them up than it'd taken to dig the holes in the first place. He'd tried thawing a hundred-pound chunk at a bonfire; at the end of eight hours, the heat hadn't penetrated two inches.

Came the day that work started on the setting of poles. Houghton, Borton, and Norman, beside the hole nearest the powerhouse, lifted the small end of a thirty-five-foot pole. Houghton held it on his shoulder while the other two got pikes into it and heaved it upright, its butt in the crater. A minute later, three pikes, their butts set firmly in frozen snow, became a tripod that held the pole in place.

Gazing at that naked pole, dark and stark against the drab, wintry sky, Houghton felt absurd. There they were—three men looking up at a cedar pole, one side of which was caked with ice, standing out of a preposterously exaggerated excavation. He pictured a line of seventy-five such poles, all held up by improvised tripods, all leaning this way and that as the heavy wires were lifted to their crossarms.

Wild ideas for filling the holes marched through Joe's mind. He thought of pouring concrete around their bases Even if concrete could be mixed in sub-zero weather, it'd cost more than the job could stand. He thought of hauling rocks to pack around the poles' bases—only to recall that there were no rocks available. With a sense of futility, he went to the trading post to talk to MacKenzie.

The old Scotsman was kind, but firm. He said:

"Ye're good, hard-working lads, but ye're no familiar with the north country. Ye've attempted an impossible job. It's me who's financing yon installation, and I tell ye to postpone further work until spring. 'Twill cost your boss financial loss, o' course, but that canna be helped. The road to outside will be opened one o' these days, an' ye can go home an' wait until the thaw. I'm tellin' ye that ye canna fill those holes satisfactorily in the winter."

"We'll fill them," Houghton said.

"Aye?" MacKenzie asked. "An' will ye tell me how?"

"I don't know, yet, but we'll do it."

"Ye're verra sure."

"Yes, sir. I'm sure."

"I tell ye that ye're foolish. How can ye be sure?"

"I pray about things."

MacKenzie's eyes caught fire beneath ragged gray brows. "Whoosh! Ye've fair floored me, lad. If ye're a praying man, ye'll get the job done." He pulled at his beard. "Go ahead, lad. I'll no interfere between ye an' God."

That night Houghton prayed again. He wakened in the morning with a full-blown plan in his mind. He went to MacKenzie and said:

"We'll fill those holes with water, sir. It'll freeze quickly, and hold the poles as solidly as if they were in granite. We'll come back again at spring thawing, and fill the holes with earth."

MacKenzie's eyes crinkled. "I'll put no worries in your path, lad. The idea's fine—if it works. Where will ye get the water? How will ye get it to the holes? Ye'll need a lot of that water, an' there isna a deep well anywhere that can supply it. However, go ahead if ye believe God has advised it. I'll no hold up your boss's money. I'll accept your word that ye'll come back an' tamp in the poles as they should be."

Houghton explained his scheme to Borton and Norman. They grinned. They scouted the town until they found an abandoned 100-gallon oil drum, rolled it to Petrie's shop and told him to fit it with a four-inch faucet and then attach the drum to one of the bobsleds so it could be used to haul water.

They took axes, and plodded three miles across snow to a

spot where the Swan River ran deep. Two full days later, they'd chopped and hacked a hole through six feet of ice. Below, water ran coldly black. They rigged a hand pump and kept it thawed with a blowtorch.

With two bobsleds, they drove back and forth through the drifts until they'd packed a usable road. Then they filled the tank with water, and with harness bells jingling, raced for the lone pole standing beside the powerhouse. They drew the sled to the dynamited crater and tried to open the faucet. The faucet was frozen tight. A blowtorch thawed it, and water, first a trickle, then a stream, gurgled into the big hole. Before the tank was empty, the hole was half-filled.

Back they raced for more water, and when they returned, ice had already darkened the surface of the water in the hole. Half an hour after the crater'd been filled, the pikes were withdrawn, and the pole stood securely in hardening ice.

Setting up the poles and filling the holes became a game. Back and forth between river and line, the bobsled jangled. Even the horses seemed to catch the spirit, and pranced in impatience when the sled was standing still.

Pete Petrie, laughing and joking, came to help. Bob Elliott, who ran the pool hall, showed up, and with Petrie and Houghton, began hoisting poles into position. Shortly after noon one day, Trader MacKenzie, followed by half the town-folk, mushed out to watch the fun. The sun set at 3:30, but work went on by the light of lanterns twinkling and flashing along the course of the power line.

The next day, and the next, the party continued. When every pole was frozen solidly in place, the men, with steel climbers on moccasined feet, went up the poles, straddled the crossarms, let down lengths of light wire to be attached to heavy feeders that lay along the ground. Hand over hand, conductors were pulled up and laid across the crossarms inside the insulators. The wires dangled in long, graceful loops between poles.

Horses were hitched to the ends of the feeders. They leaned against their collars. Their caulked shoes dug into the snow, and the horses pulled hard. As they moved forward, the low-hanging loops rose, shallowed, and were suddenly straight, tight, parallel lines. Up and down the poles raced Houghton, Borton and Norman, tying the big wires into insulators.

The next day while Borton and Norman connected house leads, Houghton hooked up the line to the switchboard. Three days before Christmas, they started the big Y-type engine. Its exhaust boomed hollowly in the great barrel in which it had been buried.

Houghton stood by the main switch at six o'clock that night. Residents of the post were gathered in the street in front of MacKenzie's store. Suddenly the engine's exhaust took on a deeper tone, and voices of the crowd were hushed. Houghton was turning up the rheostat, easing the load onto the line.

The engine sang its song of power. The aurora, so bright in the black sky a moment before, seemed to pale as windows in stores and houses blazed white from the lights within. The crowd murmured, and the murmur became a roar.

With God's help, Joe Houghton had brought light to Fort Pelly for Christmas.

MY LIFE holds many incidents as remarkable as that in "Christmas Eve Miracle." Not long ago I was writing an article on the meaning of the word "God." I knew that in many countries "God" is synonymous with "Good," but I felt there was a deeper meaning, and vainly tried to find it. Finally I stopped puzzling about it, certain that if there was a further definition, it would be revealed to me.

A few days later my wife handed me a paperback book—one I'd never heard of. The title didn't interest me so I put the book on a shelf, and went to bed.

Toward morning I wakened, impelled to look at that book. I opened it at random. The word "gheu" in italics caught my eye, and I read that "gheu" is the ancient Aryan root word for God. This didn't help much, for the book didn't give the Aryan definition.

On the same shelf was an old copy of the New English Dictionary. I opened it—and there it was! "Gheu," meaning "to pray."

Christmas Eve Miracle

ONE CHRISTMAS EVE, when I was a police reporter on the Seattle *Post Intelligencer,* I was idling at my typewriter in the police station press room when an overwhelming impulse sent me hurrying to Pioneer Square, three blocks down the street, where I arrived just in time to knock a loaded revolver away from the head of a man about to shoot himself.

A cold drizzle was falling, and the gun slid across the glistening path and came to rest in the grass. The little park was deserted. For an unreal moment, I stared at the illuminated hands of a clock in the window of a restaurant across the street. They read five minutes past seven.

Three or four minutes ago, I'd been half-dozing in the warm, poorly-ventilated reporters' room. Now here I was at the foot of Seattle's Skid Row with a man I'd just saved from death.

Whence had come the impulse that sent me out into the dreary night? What had directed me to the exact spot where a fellow-human was about to blast himself into eternity? It seemed so fantastic that I wondered if I was dreaming. However, I didn't have time to think much about it for the man suddenly dropped to his knees and began fumbling in the wet grass for the gun.

I pushed him with my foot, and he sprawled on his face. I picked up the gun and slipped it into my coat pocket. Then I helped the man to his feet. He was blubbering.

"Snap out of it, fellow," I said. "I'm here to help you. Let's go across to that restaurant and get some hot soup, or something."

He didn't answer. I put my hand on his shoulder.

"For God's sake," he said, "go away. Leave me alone." Then he covered his face with his hands.

Rain was running down the back of my neck, and I pulled up my coat collar. "Come on, Jack. Snap out of it," I said.

He looked at me. "You know me?" he asked.

"No."

"You called me *Jack*."

"Okay, Jack. Let's go someplace where it's dry. Someplace where we can talk."

He shook his head. "I don't want to talk," he said. But he did want to talk, for words began pouring from him.

"I can't go on," he said. "I can't face them. They have no food. No Christmas presents. I'm tired and sick. I'm in hell."

"Who are *they?*" I said.

"My family. My wife and kids. I've walked these streets for six days with that stuff," he said, pointing to a square bundle lying on the walk. "Stuff to prevent windshields fogging," he explained. "I've been trying to sell it. Six days. Know how much I've made? Seventy-five cents."

"How about that soup now, Jack?" I said.

"Yes . . . Jack," he said bitterly. "Jack Bryan—Auto Accessories. Know what? The constable locked the doors of my business last week. Didn't even let me take the money from the till. Finance company took my car. No money. No food in the house. I picked up this line of windshield stuff to sell. Six days. Seventy-five cents. Going crazy with worry. I saw that gun in a service station, and stole it. No food in the house. No money for rent. Six days . . ."

"Yes, yes, Jack," I interrupted—for he was becoming incoherent. He was cold and wet; probably hungry. I walked him across First Street to a restaurant.

We never did get that soup. Inside the restaurant, I went to a pay phone and called my city editor. He ordered me to rush over to the morgue and ride out with the "dead wagon" to pick up the body of a woman reported murdered.

Grabbing Bryan by the arm, I hurried him up an alley and into the morgue garage. Bill Corson, son of the City Coroner, was in the driver's seat. We piled in beside him and rolled out into the night.

Bryan didn't seem to know or to care what was happening. He sat there next to me, hunched and silent. I handed him two ten-dollar bills, but he pushed them aside, so I crumpled them and pushed them into the breast pocket of his coat.

Corson turned left beyond King Street station, and the wagon squished through mud and slush into Seattle's worst slum district—a section where poverty-stricken Italians lived in squalor. We pulled up before a ramshackle house over-flowing with wailing, moaning neighbors. Corson and I carried the basket, and Bryan followed.

We set the basket on the floor in a small bedroom in which the body of a large, work-worn woman lay on a broken-down bed. She hadn't been murdered—she'd dropped dead at her washtub.

Corson ushered the neighbors into the yard. The woman's husband and five small children remained at the foot of the bed, clutching one another.

I'll never forget the misery in that husband's eyes. Bryan noticed it too, for as Corson and I lifted the heavy body into the basket, he walked to the man, and without a word, handed him one of the two ten-dollar bills I'd put in his pocket.

The husband sobbed, and the children began a sympathetic lament. Corson strapped down the lid, and we carried the basket through the mob of neighbors in the yard, and lifted it into the wagon.

As the three of us settled into the front seat, Bryan said, "I've got to get home. Please—take me home. I must have been crazy. I didn't know what misery is."

Corson swung around to James Street and dropped Bryan and me off in front of a small white cottage. Bryan hurried up the steps. I followed, slowly. I paused in the little hall and watched through the kitchen door. With eyes closed, Bryan was holding his wife as if he'd never let her go. Two little girls, about three and five years old, were each hugging one of their daddy's legs.

Then Mrs. Bryan noticed me, and moved out of her husband's arms. She came into the hall, and shut the door. "He's been so worried and sick," she said, eyes filled with tears. "Tonight when he wasn't home by seven o'clock, I knelt down and prayed God to please take care of him, and to bring him home safely. And here he is."

I realized then, why the impulse to get to Pioneer Square had come to me at exactly seven. I felt awed and humble.

"His business went broke," Mrs. Bryan said, "but I'm not a bit worried. I've asked God to take care of that, too."

I looked into Mrs. Bryan's calm eyes and thought: It was this woman's faith in God that sent me out into this dismal night to bring her husband home to her.

I said, "I'm certain things will work out just as you want them to, Mrs. Bryan."

I told her to call me at the police station if she needed me, then stepped out onto the little porch. As the door closed behind me, I remembered that Bryan had given ten dollars to the Italian, so I turned back into the house. Father, mother, and the two little girls were kneeling at kitchen chairs, praying. I stood for a moment, then tiptoeing to the table put a few one-dollar bills on it and slipped out.

God did take care of Bryan's business. Today, automobile men up and down the Pacific Coast know Jack Bryan, and his line of accessories.

Back at the police station press room, I picked up the phone and called the city desk. "That trip with Corson," I said.

"I'll give you a rewrite man," said the city editor.

"No—don't bother," I said. "There wasn't any story."

THE AFRICAN native missionary, Sehemo—better known as Letwaba—was the most effective black preacher that Africa has ever had. Feeling called to bring the Word of God to native tribes of Northern Transvaal, he walked many hundreds of toilsome miles, preaching and teaching as he went. He had no money, no shoes; faced hostile tribes on the veldt and in the brush. He was stoned, and beaten with sticks, but never once did he falter in faith.

Prayer was his bulwark, his sword and shield. He prayed for the soul-sick and the physically sick, and healings followed to such an extent that in time thousands of natives, from many tribes, learned to live as Jesus would have them do.

Letwaba, who was one of my missionary father's converts, is the central figure in a book, When God Makes a Pastor, *written by W. F. P. Burton, published in England.*

About prayer, Letwaba once said:

"The urge to pray is itself a prayer. The act of praying brings God into your mind. When God is in your mind, He makes you think true. When you think true, all the gifts of God become yours for the taking." *

* Translation from M'Shangaan.

The Gray Ox and the Lions

THIS IS THE story of Bill McLain, of Oakland, California, a young, headstrong, impatient man who almost lost his faith in God because his business failed despite his rayers; who tried to induce God to help him put over an nsound business proposition; and who found, when wallowng in what he thought was financial and spiritual disaster, that in reality his feet had been placed on the road to success.

Early in 1950 Bill had gone to work as a salesman for a company manufacturing calculating machines. They were flashy articles, made to undersell competitive lines, and Bill had brought in some nice business. Because the plant was just getting into production, the orders were for future delivery.

In April the company ran short of money, and applied to the State Corporation Commissioner for a permit to issue more stock. The commissioner refused the permit until all of the company's debts were paid.

Shortly afterward, Bill was called into the president's office and offered the job of sales manager, provided he bought $10,000 worth of stock. Bill didn't have $10,000, but he raised $2,500 with which he bought an option on the shares.

That night Bill knelt at his bedside and asked God to help him make good.

A month of hard work followed. Bill made no sales. Three months went by—still no sales.

Bill's prayers became insistent. Nothing happened. His prayers became despairing pleas, but no sales materialized. Then he stopped praying.

In August, the night before his option was to expire, Bill came to my home, a sick man.

"I'm going to lose my shirt," he said. "I need $7,500 to pick up my option before noon tomorrow. The banks have turned me down. The loan companies have turned me down. My friends have turned me down. My own father has turned me down." His voice grew querulous: "And God turned me down too."

"Nonsense," I said. "God doesn't turn down those who ask His aid, if their cause is right."

Bill's reply was almost petulant: "But God has ignored my prayers, I tell you. I've not made one sale since I began praying."

"If God hasn't answered your prayers," I said, "then there's something wrong with your prayers—or with you, Bill."

Bill flared up. "Who are you to tell me a thing like that? I'm as good a Christian as you are—as anybody." His anger ebbed as quickly as it had risen. Despairingly, he said, "But something *is* wrong—terribly wrong. I feel lost—lost." He put his face in his hands and I saw that his fingers were trembling.

"My head aches," he said.

I sat looking at him, wishing I could help him. He was a likeable fellow even though stubborn, hotheaded, and unimaginative. Bill would have his own way, or smash up in the attempt. Suddenly, out of the dim past, I remembered something. The memory surprised me into saying aloud, "Sehemo's gray ox."

Bill looked up, hurt: "Ox? You mean me?"

I went into my study, took an old scrapbook from a shelf,

went back to Bill and handed him the book. "Read this," I
said, pointing to a clipping. "It's about that ox."
Bill pushed the book aside. "I don't feel like reading—I
want to borrow $7,500. That's all I'm interested in."
"Years ago, Bill," I said, "I was an African correspondent
for the *London Daily Mail*. Among articles of mine published in that newspaper was a series on native churches.
One of the outstanding native ministers of that time was a
big Zulu named Oliphant Sehemo. He based his ministry almost entirely on the words of Jesus. He told me that Jesus'
teachings were so clear, simple and appealing that his own
artless, untutored congregation readily understood them and
loved them.

"Sehemo, like Jesus, frequently taught in parables, using
illustrations that were within the experiences of his people.
He tried to make his points by talking as he thought Jesus
might talk if He were speaking to Zulus in the Zulu lan-
guage."

Bill said: "So?"

"This clipping," I said, "is a report of one of Sehemo's
sermons. Zulus are chiefly husbandmen. Their principal
means of transportation is the ox wagon. Usually sixteen
oxen are yoked in pairs to make up a span; but when mountains are to be crossed with heavy loads, it's not unusual to
use forty-eight or fifty oxen. For a driver to keep that many
beasts, each with a different temperament, working together,
pulling together, straining together, requires skill and patience. Most Zulus are excellent oxen drivers.

"On a Sunday morning, when I was the only white man
in a little corrugated-iron church in northern Natal, Sehemo
used oxen to illustrate his message."

"Okay," Bill said, "let's see the clipping." He read
Sehemo's sermon to himself, silently.

Some of you, my children, tell me that you pray, but get no answers. You tell me that you ask and ask, but God turns away His ear. You tell me that you have great faith, because you are good men, but still, God does not hear you.

You tell me that you refrain from swearing, from stealing, from committing adultery, from coveting your neighbors' belongings.

I tell you that your prayers are not answered because the love of God is not in them. You tell God how good you are. Then you lie around the *mealie* pots waiting for Him to give you things as *bansela* (reward). You obey the Old Testament commandments, but you forget that Jesus gave us two new commandments. They tower above all others, as yonder mountain towers above the *veldt*. Listen:

"And thou shalt love the Lord thy God with all thy heart, and with all thy soul, and with all thy strength."

The second commandment is this:

"Thou shalt love thy neighbor as thyself. There is none other commandment greater than these."

Hear me, my children! You are like oxen. God is your driver. The road is rutty, stony, winding, scored. It climbs steeply toward the distant peak of the wind-tortured mountain. It dips into mudholes. The oxen slip. Their hoofs make grooves in the mud. The road hangs on the edge of a cliff. To fall means death on the rocks far below. The wagon skids, and slides toward the edge of the cliff. It stops. The oxen tremble. The driver speaks to them, calling each by name. He speaks gently, encouragingly. He talks them into leaning against their yokes, all together, all as one.

The driver says: "Pull, my sons. We must reach the summit and get down into the warm valley on the other side before the night comes with its purple thunders; before the winds rise shrieking, and the rain makes our road a torrent. Pull, my sons, with all your hearts, with all your souls, with all your minds, with all your strength."

The oxen strain. They bow their backs. The wagon creaks. It moves. It rolls. The driver walks up and down beside the span. He pats an ox here, and another there. He encourages all. He praises their sturdy efforts.

At last he lets the span pause to rest beside a road that winds off to the left. It has an easy grade, and the grass that grows along it seems green and moist. In the span is a young ox, a gray one. He turns toward the left-hand road. He tries to pull his yokemate with him. The driver tries to soothe him. But the young ox sees only the easy way. He tries to break from the span. He jerks at his yoke chain. He falls. He struggles to rise, and his long horns tangle in his neighbor's yoke strap. All is confusion.

Gently the driver pats the wayward ox. He says: "You have not learned to obey—to trust me to know the best way to go. Until you learn, we must get along without you, for the night comes, and we must get to the fruitful valley."

He unyokes the gray ox, and says: "Follow us, or remain behind, as you choose. We can let you delay us no longer."

The gray ox turns down the easy road, but the wagon, drawn by the faithful oxen, creaks steadily up the hill. The gray ox bawls in protest at being left alone. There is no answer. He turns, and follows the wagon, still bawling.

The summit is reached just as shadow falls upon the eastern slopes. But westward through the pass shines the copper-red sun, spreading his comfort over the wide, grassy valley far below. The driver sets the wagon brakes, and the load rolls easily down, down into the valley floor with its knee-high grass and clear, cooling waters.

The oxen graze until shadows fall, and are then driven into a thorn *boma* that has been prepared for their protection against night-prowling lions and hyenas. The gate is shut, and the faithful oxen lie down to rest, scratching their backs with the points of their long horns. But the gray ox stands with his head over the gate. He sees the darkness creeping across the plain. He sees the shadows blacken beneath the thorn trees. But the grass is high, and he bawls to be let out. He pushes at the gate. Again he stands bawling, entreating his master to let him go forth into the danger.

The driver hears the bellowing, but he does not answer.

It comes to me, O foolish ones, that you have been bawling for the Master to let you out among the lions.

Bill finished reading. "Interesting," he said. "Do I get the loan?"

"No, Bill," I said. "I'm sorry, but I sense something wrong in your deal with that company. No loan."

I heard no more of Bill McLain for six months. Then I read in a newspaper that the president of his company, and two of the promoters, had been indicted on charges of fraud, infringement of patents, and failure to comply with the ruling of the corporation commissioner.

That evening I got Bill on the telephone at his home. He said:

"I've been intending to call you, but one thing and another came up . . ."

"I know," I said. "Are you in the clear in that company mess?"

"I thought you knew," he said. "The day after I saw you, I forfeited my option money, and quit the company." He laughed as though embarrassed. "You know," he said, "I didn't like that ox story very well, but in bed that night, I couldn't get it out of my mind. Before morning I realized that I, too, had been bawling at a gate—asking God to let me out among the lions. Things are well with me now."

"What are you doing now, Bill?"

"Selling calculating machines for another company—a good one. But I don't high-pressure for sales any more. I try to find out if, and how, my machine will benefit my prospect. I think of him as my neighbor. Sales seem to follow as a matter of course. Also, I've stopped trying to tell God how to answer my prayers. And to remind me of how foolish I used to be, I keep something on my desk that Sehemo would have appreciated."

"Yes?"

Bill chuckled. "A small model of a young gray ox," he said.

"HAVING read Mr. Moray's somewhat unorthodox presentation of the curing of his alcoholism," says Psychiatrist Victor M. Reich, "I am constrained to admit that in designating confirmed alcoholics and gamblers as chiefly individuals who live on a childhood emotional level, he is stating a truth. His claims for the part prayer can play in a cure are in line with modern psychiatric thought.

"There is a growing belief among psychologists that not sex nor will-to-power, but the search for God, is humanity's most powerful drive. And Dr. C. G. Jung has stated that the need of a religious outlook is the basic need of all of his patients past the age of thirty-five."

There Are No Hopeless Alcoholics

WHEN ATTORNEY GEORGE MORAY came out of a two-weeks-long alcoholic fog, he was in bed in a room in San Francisco's Palace Hotel. It was early morning, and a too-cool breeze blew in through a wide-open window. Moray swung his feet over the edge of the bed and sat trying to work up enough energy to close the window. An empty whiskey bottle lay in front of the dresser. Two exhausted soda-water siphons, and three drinking glasses containing watered dregs, stood in a puddle of spilled whiskey on the telephone stand. Holding his hands in front of him, Moray watched them tremble.

He tried to pull the window down, found the slight task too much, and stood staring down at traffic six floors below. Nearly overwhelmed by a sudden impulse to jump, he staggered into the bathroom and shut the door. He drew a warm bath, got into it, and immediately his heart began pounding. He got out of the tub and stood, drawing great, gulping breaths. Heartbeats shook his whole body.

He opened the bathroom door, crawled on hands and knees to the telephone stand, reached up and drained each glass of its whiskey dregs. Then still on the floor, he telephoned his home.

"Elsie," he said to his wife, "come and get me. Quickly."

"Where are you, George?"

"Palace Hotel." He replaced the receiver and got back into bed.

Elsie brought with her the family doctor. The doctor gave Moray a sedative, helped him dress, called the bar to send up a stiff drink, watched Moray gulp it, and said:

"Take him home now, Mrs. Moray, and put him to bed. Feed him lots of thin soup—hasn't eaten for a week. I'll be out to see him in a couple of hours."

At home, and in bed, Moray sipped three cups of consommé, and fell asleep. The doctor came, felt Moray's pulse, nodded, then turned to Elsie and said, "He's doing all right, Mrs. Moray. You're in worse shape than he is."

He opened the bedroom door, guided her to the sunporch and gently pushed her into a chair. Mrs. Moray began to cry. The doctor said, "You're in bad shape, Mrs. Moray. You must get away from this."

"Yes," she said tonelessly, "I can't go on, Doctor. Sometimes it's days, sometimes a week—this time, two weeks." With hands palms-up in her lap, she said:

"When he's off on a binge, I jump every time the phone rings, every time there's a knock at the door. I picture him bleeding and broken in an accident, lying in a jail cell or brawling in some dive. The children are tense and ashamed, hoping he'll not humiliate them by staggering drunkenly down the street. Both children, Doctor, are in trouble at school—some sort of reaction to their father's drinking. When George does finally come home, they leave the house by the back door, or lock themselves in their rooms. Henry's thirteen now, and Lucille's eleven—sensitive ages. When George shows up high and happy, it seems even worse, for then he jokes with them, and when they don't respond as he thinks they should, he flies into cursing rages."

She wiped tears from her eyes and went on. "During the first day or two of a drunk, he buys all sorts of presents for us—beautiful underthings and nightgowns for me—dresses for Lucille—books for Henry. He puts the gifts on the back seat of his car, and they're soon on the floor. His car is crowded with drunken friends, and they trample the presents, spill liquor on them—ruin them.

"Sometimes he buys foods—cakes, pies, turkeys, boxes of candy—all ruined like the other things."

She stood up abruptly. The doctor said, "Sit down, Mrs. Moray. It's good to talk. Relieves tension." She sank into the chair.

"Sometimes he buys chickens—live ones. Puts them in the trunk of the car—forgets them. They die. The smell . . ."

"Go on," the doctor urged.

"Sometimes he comes home in an amorous mood . . ." She put a hand to her throat and looked at the doctor, wildly. "What can I do? Dear God, what can I do?"

"Commit him to a state institution, Mrs. Moray."

"He won't go."

"The court would commit him for you."

"Would commitment cure his drinking?"

"No—probably not, but it'd benefit him physically, and give you time to regain some balance."

"I'll do it, Doctor," Elsie said, and wept again softly.

"I'll commit myself," Moray said from the doorway. "Today."

Elsie accompanied her husband to the District Attorney's office, signed commitment papers, then drove him one hundred miles to the State Hospital at Mendocino. A house physician took them to his office, where Elsie said "goodbye," and watched her husband led away by an attendant. As George disappeared around a bend in the corridor, Elsie felt a surprising sense of relief. The man she loved would be a prisoner for six months—and she was glad, yet her heart ached.

In the months that followed Mrs. Moray visited her husband as often as possible, and each time left with increased confidence that he'd be cured. Moray's physician warned her not to be too optimistic, but she smiled at the warning. Hadn't George told her he'd had his lesson—was through with liquor for life?

Very soon after Moray's commitment, Henry's school troubles vanished, and his work improved. Lucille's progress was slower. The fact that her father was in Mendocino Hospital was known to friends and neighbors, and the little girl's humiliation was deep. In time, however, she too became a happier, more normal schoolchild. Near the end of Moray's incarceration, the entire little family looked forward eagerly to his release.

EXACTLY SIX MONTHS AFTER he'd been admitted, Moray was discharged from the hospital. On the way out, he paused at the institution's front door to stare across acres of vines laden with purple grapes against a background of dark-green, drowsing hills. Then to a passing attendant he said, "So long, Joe."

Joe shook hands. "I'll be seeing you, Mr. Moray."

"You'll never see me *here* again, Joe," Moray said. "You've done a good job on me. I don't even have a thirst. I'm off the stuff for life."

"They always come back," Joe said morosely, "but good luck anyway, Mr. Moray."

Moray got off the hospital bus in front of the garage in Ukiah where Elsie'd left his car on her last visit. She'd have liked driving him home herself, but had been told it was better for him to have that hour or two of driving to adjust himself.

The garageman said the car needed servicing, so Moray walked across the street to a drugstore, and telephoned Elsie.

"Darling!" she said.

"I'll be home in two hours, Elsie," he told her. "Let me talk to the kids."

His car was parked at the curb, ready. He paid the bill, got into the car, but instead of starting the engine, he sat, both hands on the wheel, suddenly brooding. He thought:

Tomorrow I'll be back at the office. It's in bad shape. Lost most of my clients, I imagine. Finances are low. Suppose I'll have to put up with snide references from some people. I've always hated that office. Now it'll be worse.

Next to the garage a neon sign glowed, casting a green reflection from the gray hood of his car. Moray glanced up at the sign: *Tavern!*

Moray started to sweat, and his heart began thumping. He stepped from the car and stood on the sidewalk. A whiff of stale spirits drifted from the tavern. Moray entered the cool, dark interior. To the bartender he said, "Double gin."

An hour later, he said thickly: "Gimme a fifth to take out. I gotta go."

"You goin' to drive your car, Bud?" the bartender asked.

"Gotta get to Frisco."

"You ain't in no shape to drive a car—but that's your business, I guess." The bartender tipped a bottle over a glass and said, "Have one for the road, Bud," then nodded to the porter, and watched while the porter went out to remove the keys from Moray's car.

Moray downed his drink, said, "Thanks," walked unsteadily to his car, got in, fumbled for the ignition key, didn't find it, pressed the self-starter button angrily, and held it down.

A motorcycle traffic officer pulled up alongside and asked, "Trouble, Mister?"

"Won't start," Moray said. "Gotta get to Frisco."

"Let's see your driver's license, please."

Trying to get a hand in his back pants pocket, Moray leaned too far over, and sprawled on the seat. The officer helped him sit up, then said, "You're drunk, Mister. Can't let you drive a car."

"Nuts," Moray said, and swung a punch.

The officer parked his motorcycle at the curb, took the car keys from the tavern porter who stood watching, pushed Moray over, and got behind the wheel. He inserted the key, started the motor and said:

"I'll drive you, Mister."

A few minutes later, George Moray was in a jail cell charged with "being drunk in an automobile."

Next morning Moray paid a fine, and immediately headed for a bar, and a few quick ones. As he drank, his feeling of guilt slowly changed to one of resentment against his family.

"It's by that type of perverse reasoning that many alcoholics justify their actions," Moray told me during an interview. "By the time I'd downed my second drink that morning, I was thinking like this:

"*Those drinks yesterday afternoon hit me hard because I've been off the stuff for six months. Normally, they'd not have affected me like that. Elsie won't understand that after my hospital ordeal it'll be difficult to face up to things at the office. Trouble with me is that I dislike legal work—shrink from it. Drinks bolster me. It's only a question of not taking too many. If I were single, I'd not have to get right back into the grind. I could go to some hideaway and stay there long enough to get in the mood for work. But finances are low, and the family needs money. Money, money, money—always money. If I didn't have the family . . .*

"I bought a pint. I knew Elsie'd greet me with a forced smile; that Henry and Lucille wouldn't be able to hide the reproach in their eyes. It'd be difficult to face them, so just before turning into our street, I killed the pint. It gave me a lift, and made me feel like a man instead of a mouse. I greeted them, then went to my room, lay down on my bed, and listened to kitchen sounds downstairs. Elsie was preparing special foods for a home-coming celebration. I smiled, and fell asleep.

"I wakened at dusk with a dark-brown taste in my mouth, and a renewed feeling of guilt. I needed a drink, so slipped out a side door, walked to the nearest bar, met a couple of cronies, and arrived home at three o'clock next morning—singing merrily.

"Around noon I went down to the kitchen in my pajamas to get a snack. There seemed to be no one in the house, so I helped myself from the refrigerator. There was a note on the kitchen table.

> "George:
> There's a limit even for those who love, so the children and I are leaving. We've deserved better than you've given us, and now we're going to try to find those better things for ourselves. I've a job to go to, so don't worry about us. Perhaps someday you'll make it possible for us to come back to you. We love you, George—love you dearly, but we must go, or be destroyed.
>   Elsie.
> "P.S. Oh, darling.

"I read the note over and over, but for a while all that sunk in were the words: 'the children and I are leaving.'

"Finally I noticed I'd left the refrigerator door open. I closed it, went to the pantry, found my last bottle of Scotch, uncorked it, tipped it over a glass, abruptly changed my mind and poured the liquor down the sink. I said aloud:

" 'That does it. I've taken my last drink.'

"During the next two hours, I suffered as only an alcoholic

who's kicked everything out from under himself can suffer. I was sick with remorse, and an overpowering sense of loss. I needed a drink, but had there been one available, and had I been willing to take it, I couldn't have done so—for I was filled with intense hatred against the thing that had destroyed me.

"Then I began feeling sorry for myself, and the more I pitied myself, the more I resented being deserted. Again, by an alcoholic's strange reasoning, I began to see myself as a good guy who'd been let down by those he loved and trusted. My thoughts ran like this:

"*My drinking was a weakness—one I was born with. But I could have whipped it. If Elsie'd waited . . . Well, she hadn't. She'd gone off without giving me a chance to prove I really meant to quit. I'd intended to tell her I'd stop drinking just as soon as I felt better able to go back to the office. True, I've made things difficult for the family, but it's a poor family that can't put up with occasional lapses. Elsie married me for better or for worse. What if it had been getting a little on the worse side? She should have stuck things out. If I fall off the wagon again, it'll be Elsie's fault. She'd no right to leave me to fight things out alone. Okay, if that's the way she wanted it, that's the way it'll be . . .*

"At last, having convinced myself that I was abused and neglected, I cursed the family, went to the telephone, called a liquor store and ordered six fifths of bourbon delivered. I stayed in the house, and killed all six bottles in four days.

"During the next twelve months, I went completely to pieces. I sold my law practice, and drank the money up. I sold my car, and drank up that money, too. I'd have sold the house, but that was in Elsie's name, and without her consent I could make no deal. Anyway, I didn't know where Elsie was. In time, funds ran out, so I began drinking Skid Row muscatel and sherry—deadly stuff at twenty cents a quart. A month on Skid Row wine put me right into the gutter. After my eighth arrest for drunkenness, a judge with whom I'd gone to law school committed me again to Mendocino State Hospital.

"I was given work in the institution's dairy barns and I tried to accept things with good grace, but days and nights were a torture.

"One morning as I leaned on a pitchfork, brooding, an aged Catholic priest who'd come to visit one of his parishioners—an alcoholic—paused beside me and said:

" 'You seem troubled, my son.'

" 'Skip it, Father,' I answered.

" 'Are you a mental patient?'

" 'No. An alcoholic—a hopeless one.'

" 'Do you dare use the word *hopeless?*'

" 'I've lost everything,' I said.

" 'Still, it's not hopeless. My son, *there is no such thing as a hopeless alcoholic.* I've been working with men like you for more than fifty years. I've never yet known a hopeless case. Nothing is hopeless so long as God's in His Heaven.'

"I didn't answer. He went on:

" 'Your way may be dark, and your mountains of fear yet to be crossed, but God—if you ask Him—will guide you safely to the valleys of peace that lie on the other side. You must pray, my son.'

" 'Pray for what?'

" 'Pray for maturity of mind,' he said.

" 'Oh, twaddle,' I snapped.

" 'You'll see me here at the barns quite often,' he said. 'We'll have further talks. In the meantime, pray, my son. And never forget that there are no incurable alcoholics.'

" 'What did you mean by *maturity of mind?*' I asked.

" 'I meant you should pray that God will help you grow beyond the emotional level of your childhood.'

"Before I could speak, Father Ferraris said:

" 'Don't resent those words, my son. I've seen the agony of your soul. You drift without an anchor—tossed by waves of despair—with no rock to cling to. These things need not be, my son. Learn to pray, and you'll reach safe harbor.'

"The old priest's eyes were warm, and his voice mellow with sympathy. My antagonism vanished. I said, 'I'm here in a mental institution as an alcoholic, but I'll be a mental case before long, Father. I've kicked everything I've built out from under me. This place offers no cure—only an interlude between drunks. Nights are hell, and days not much better. I tell you . . .'

"My voice held a note of hysteria, and Father Ferraris held up a hand. 'Listen calmly, my son. For many years I've been helping alcoholics—hundreds of them. Many were once as despairing as you. They listened, prayed, and one by one, were healed of the infirmities that caused them to drink. Among them were doctors, lawyers, businessmen, laborers, artists, community leaders. They became whole, and not only rebuilt their own lives, but devoted themselves to helping others in whom drink had extinguished hope.'

" 'Psychiatrists,' I said, 'have been trying to uncover conflicts to explain why I drink. No luck.'

" 'Well, my son,' the old priest said, 'I know about conflicts, suppressions, complexes, compulsions, and all the rest of it, too. But understanding such things is beside the point. Your recovery will come when you see yourself as you really are.' Father Ferraris took off his hat, wiped his bald spot with a large red handkerchief, and went on slowly and impressively:

" 'You're an alcoholic, my son, because your emotional development was arrested somewhere back in your childhood —at the age when all children are self-centered—selfish. All the alcoholics I've known—without a single exception—were

emotionally, or mentally, immature. The moment they began to strive toward maturity—with God's help—alcoholism
was no longer their problem.'

" 'Okay,' I said testily, 'I'm a spoiled brat, if you say so.
But tell me, Father, if you can, what is maturity?'

" 'A mature man thinks of others before himself,' the
priest answered.

" 'Go on,' I said, "let's hear the rest of it.'

" 'That's all there is, my son,' he said, and repeated: 'A
mature man thinks of others before himself.'

" 'And you think I'm immature?'

" 'I do.'

" 'Self-centered?'

" 'Yes.'

" 'Selfish?'

" 'I think so, yes.'

" 'Well,' I said, 'you're wrong, Father. The truth is . . .'

" 'Ah,' he said, 'the truth!'

"I felt suddenly uncertain—and the priest seemed so sure!

" 'I'll do some thinking about it, Father,' I said.

" 'And some praying, my son.'

" 'Yes, some praying,' I said, 'although I don't imagine
I'll be much good at it.'

" 'A childish comment.' The old man smiled and strode
away, his black robe whipping about his legs. At the barn
door he turned, smiled again, then made the sign of the cross
toward me.

"A tightness inside me suddenly loosened. I looked around
hastily, fearful that someone might see the tears in my eyes.

"A week later, when Father Ferraris showed up again at
the barn, he shook hands and asked, 'Have you prayed, my
son?'

" 'Every time I try to pray,' I said, 'all I can think of is a
prayer I said when a kid.'

" 'What did you pray then? Repeat it for me.'

" 'God bless Papa, Mama, Aunt Lizzie, Uncle Peter, Rover, the cows, the horses, the chickens, and everybody in the world.'

" 'That is a fine prayer, my son,' Father Ferraris said. 'You prayed for others then—didn't even mention yourself. Your selfishness must have developed later.'

" 'Look, Father,' I said, 'I feel kindly toward you—a Catholic priest who troubles himself about a Protestant—but you're wrong about me. I'm not self-centered and selfish.'

" 'Let's go sit for a while on that pile of hay,' he said. 'I've things to ask you.'

"After we were seated, he said, 'Repeat this little prayer after me, my son: God, help me to see myself as I am.'

"I repeated his prayer, almost resentfully.

"He said: 'So you're not self-centered and selfish!'

" 'No,' I said, 'I'm over-generous, really. Always have been.'

" 'For example?'

" 'I often lent money to people in trouble, sometimes too much money.'

" 'Just so. Made your own finances pretty short at times. Forced your family, I suppose, to sometimes do without things they needed.'

" 'Well . . . not at first, but later, the stores shut off credit, and . . .'

" 'Family went without things, eh? Short on food sometimes?'

" 'Look, Father. When the family was short on food occasionally, so was I short on it. A family should . . .'

" 'You went without liquor at those times?'

" 'Well, no. I needed . . .'

" 'Needed alcoholic stimulation to tide you over such financial doldrums?'

" 'Well, yes.'

" 'I see. Family went short on food and clothes, but you never went short on liquor. Probably drank more than usual at such times, eh?'

" 'Well . . .'

" 'Somebody made sacrifices so you could lend that money, my son. Who?'

" 'Well, if you look at it that way . . .' I paused, flustered.

" 'Speak true, my son. Who really lent those sums?'

" 'I see what you mean—my family.'

" 'But you got some sort of personal satisfaction from being a big-hearted philanthropist, eh? Made your ego swell and strut, eh?'

" 'Doggone it, Father . . .'

" 'Answer true, my son.'

" 'I guess I *was* selfish in those cases,' I said, 'but I *thought* I was being . . . Darn it, Father, you make me feel like a boob.'

" 'You ran bills that you didn't pay. Grocery store credit shut off. Other credit shut off. You went out on long drunks. Stayed at good hotels, I suppose. Ate good meals in good restaurants, what? Drank hearty. Family sometimes live on bread and beans?'

" 'How do you know that, Father?'

" 'Bread and beans are often the chief diet of alcoholics' families. I wonder, my son, if while on one of your binges, you ever thought of sending some cash home by messenger?'

" 'Stop it,' I shouted, springing to my feet. 'I'm not as bad as you make out. I worried about my family—lots of times. Worrying about my family was one of the things that made me drink.' I sat down again. 'Sorry, Father,' I said, 'but you're making me appear a heel, and I'm not. I mean . . .'

" 'Didn't pay your family's bills promptly, eh?'

" 'Not toward the end. Truth is, I didn't pay *any* bills during the last year or so that my family was with me. Couldn't cut it. Business dropping off, and all.'

" 'Gamble much?'

" 'I like the horses. Always a chance of making a killing to pull myself out of the hole.'

" 'Ever make a killing?'

" 'Well, the books don't pay off at track prices, but even at that, I had some good days.'

" 'Used your winnings to pay bills, I presume.'

" 'Yes—sometimes.'

" 'But not often?'

" 'No—not often.'

" 'Had credit with the bookmakers?'

" 'Sure. Made my bets by phone. Had to have credit.'

" 'Always kept that credit good? Paid off your losses promptly?'

" 'Certainly. Debts-of-honor. A man's got to pay his gambling debts.'

" 'Of course. As you say—debts-of-honor. Grocery store bills are not debts-of-honor? It's all right to let grocery bills slide?'

" 'Look, Father, you don't understand. Liquor and gambling bills *must* be paid or they cut you off at the pockets.'

" 'My son, I've been a priest for almost fifty-five years. If there's anything about the frailities of human nature that I don't understand, it's something rare, indeed. I know drunkards and gamblers as few men know them. How could I help knowing them? I've spent a great deal of my time helping the pitiful families of alcoholics and gamblers. Tell me, my son, how did your family fare during those times you were financially short after paying the debts-of-honor?'

"I jumped up again, protesting. 'I don't want to hear any more about it,' I said, and walked away from him.

"He got to his feet, smiling, and called after me: 'Who paid those debts-of-honor? You, or your family?'

" 'Go to the devil!' I cried, and hurried into the barn.

"It can be an unpleasant experience," Moray said, "for a man to come face-to-face with himself—stripped of the qualities and characteristics with which he'd endowed himself in order to bolster a sagging ego. If I'd been where I could have gotten some liquor, it—the liquor—would have stopped the self-analysis, but I wasn't. There was nothing to do but face up to things.

"For several days, my ego dodged and twisted to evade my thoughts, but that didn't work, because the priest's prayer ran through my mind constantly: *God, help me to see myself as I am.*

"Nights were particularly unhappy, for in the dark of the quiet ward, I saw things clearly. I'd always thought of myself as temperamental, because I blew up easily—shouted and cursed when crossed—was deeply resentful when criticized—stubbornly indignant when anyone suggested I might be too drunk to drive a car, or to attend to business. And now I discovered that what I'd thought was temperament, was really childishness.

"One night, with a strange shock, I realized I'd made no attempt even to locate Elsie and the children. I'd been bitter toward them for 'leaving me in the lurch.' For one full year, I'd told myself—and believed it—that I'd become a hopeless alcoholic because my family had ruined my life. Now I realized my prolonged spree had been a year-long pout. I'd been sure that when Elsie heard I was on the skids, she'd come back, remorseful and loving. By the time I realized she wasn't coming back, I'd ceased even to think of my family at all.

"In the ward with me were thirty other alcoholics. I began watching them, studying them. In the light of better understanding, I now saw that traits among them that I'd thought of as eccentricities and peculiarities, were really the reactions of infants and juveniles. One gray-haired old fellow—a family physician who'd been committed time and time again—was a hearty eater, yet when he got impatient with a waiter, or annoyed with a table-mate, he'd leave the table in a huff and go hungry until the next meal.

"Another patient—a man who'd built up a chain of fruit and vegetable stands—would sometimes push his plate of food off the table to the floor when contradicted. A musician sometimes showed resentment by tearing his bed sheets, or plugging toilet bowls. Crazy? No. Childish.

"I finally came to the conclusion that I was no worse, nor better, than they. When vexed, I cursed and shouted; the vegetable man threw his food on the floor. Different reactions—same cause: lack of maturity.

"It was nearly one month before I saw Father Ferraris again, and during that month I discovered that my ward-mates—all of them—were filled with fears and dislikes: fear of ridicule, of not being liked, of falling down on the job, of anyone in authority; dislike of jobs, of routine, of responsibility. All drank to allay their fears, and to minimize their dislikes. Most admitted they also drank when worried, irritated or bored.

"I found that 'something always started them off.' For instance, here's what they'd say:

"AN ARCHITECT'S CLERK: 'When I'm out of work, and my family's down and out, our folks send us money. When I'm sober, and earning money, the folks quit helping, and keep saying: "Now you're getting on your feet fine. Keep it up." That infuriates me—and I tumble off the wagon again.'

"A MUSICIAN: 'I'm an artist. Responsibilities interfere with my musical progress. When I'm sober, my wife insists that I perform all sorts of chores. When I'm tight, she doesn't bother me with them.'

"AN OLD FAMILY PHYSICIAN: 'I never could stand seeing others in pain. When one of my patients suffers prolonged pain, I drink to dull my feelings. Unhappily, a few drinks and I'm on a bender.'

"A WRITER: 'I'm a great playwright, really. My writings are highly emotional. It's impossible to sustain such high tension without alcohol. I drink while I'm creating. Then, when that particular bit of writing is finished, I have a letdown. Alcohol carries me over the low spot. Nobody buys my plays, naturally. All the producers want is the uninspired rot that they feed the public. I don't expect my plays to be appreciated until long after I'm dead. Alcohol helps me bear that knowledge, too.'

"A SALESMAN: 'I should be selling high-quality merchandise. Instead, I'm tied down to a line of cheap, tawdry stuff. I'm ashamed of it. And facing customers with it each day is more than I can take. A few drinks—and it's different.'

"A CONTRACTOR: 'Competition's keen, and I come home at night worn and nervous. The kids make so much noise that I go to my study with a bottle. If it weren't for those nightly snorts, I'd go nuts. The kids . . .'

"A HOUSE PAINTER: 'I have to have regular hours—I was brought up that way. I married a woman who doesn't even care about time. I like breakfast, for instance, at 6:30 sharp. Sometimes my wife doesn't have it ready until nearly seven. It makes me so nervous to wait that I slam out of the house and get a few quick ones. Sometimes when we're going someplace, she keeps me waiting in the car for twenty minutes or more while she's still in the house getting ready, or something. That makes me feel mean, so I sometimes drive off without her. I come home plastered, hoping she'll take the hint—but she never does.'

"A DENTIST: 'You'd drink too, if you had to smell fetid breaths all day.'

"A GARDENER: 'Fine weather makes me feel so cheerful and good that I just have to drink! And bad weather makes me so gloomy that I drink to cheer myself up.'

"My point in detailing those foregoing 'reasons' for some of my fellow-alcoholics' lapses," Moray explained, "is that *at one time or another, I myself, had used most of them*—and many more, equally puerile.

"Self-revelation can be a bitter thing. My own was bitter. Sick at heart, self-confidence gone, I tried to pray—but God seemed far away. As I lay tossing on my cot one night it occurred to me that since I was born an alcoholic, God was to blame—not I. I felt resentful because of that trick God had played on me. Next time I saw Father Ferraris, I asked bitterly:

" 'Why does God permit men to be born alcoholics?'

" 'He doesn't, my son,' the priest said. 'There are no born alcoholics. Alcoholism's acquired—and you well know how and why.'

" 'I can't pray,' I said. 'I can't even *think* a prayer.'

" 'One of the proofs that God exists, my son, is that Man cannot help praying. Even so-called atheists pray, although they may not realize that they do. Prayer is Man's contact with God. The only thing that can dull or diminish this contact is Man, himself. If you can't feel close to God when you pray, my son, then you're standing in your own way. What have you tried to pray for?'

" 'For myself—for strength to fight the liquor.'

" 'Only for yourself?'

" 'Well—I'm the one who most needs . . .'

" 'No prayers for your wife? Your family?'

"I was suddenly angry. 'Father,' I said, 'you're not fair.

You lay traps to make me out a culprit. No, I didn't pray for my wife. Why should I? She's quite capable of praying for herself. After all, she deserted me, remember.'

"Father Ferraris gave me a peculiar look, shrugged and walked away. I growled something after him and went back to work.

"All during supper that look of the Father's nagged at me. Later, on my cot in the darkness of the ward, I tried to maintain my antagonism toward Elsie, but memories flooded. I recalled the day I'd fallen in love with Elsie—my sense of exaltation. I recalled the evening beside a small stream when she told me she loved me, too. I remembered the light in her eyes. I recalled the plans we'd made for the future—a family. What had happened to our glorious dreams?

"A voice from the next cot said: 'You sick, fellow?'

" 'No,' I answered. 'Why?'

" 'Sounded like it. Groaning. Dreaming, I guess.'

" 'Yes,' I said, 'I've been dreaming.'

"I'd still made no attempt to get in touch with Elsie. I'd assumed she'd be all right, and that she'd have rented our house to augment her income. I prayed—this time from my heart.

" 'Dear God,' I said, 'let me see the happy light in Elsie's eyes again. Stay with me, God. Help me.'

"And clear and strong inside me, a voice said: *'Lo, I am with you always, even unto the end of the world.'*

"From somewhere deep within me had come my prayer's answer. It was deep indeed, for to this day I've no idea where or when I'd heard that passage from Matthew 28:20. I must have heard it, for I'd never read the Bible.

"I told Father Ferraris about it the next time I saw him.

" 'Remember His promise, my son,' he said, 'if you should ever again go into a saloon. God is with you always.'

" 'Yes,' I said, 'even in a saloon.'

" 'Everywhere, and always,' he said.

"THE FIRST THING I did after being discharged was to telephone Elsie's father in Sacramento.

"He told me: 'Elsie was certain you'd phone me when you were free, George, and told me to ask you not to hunt her up. Said she'd rented the house for one hundred and fifty dollars a month, and that the rent was being paid to your old law partner, who's keeping it for you—a stake for when you got home. You'll have enough to begin law practice again, George, if you're economical.'

" 'I've got to see Elsie,' I said, 'I've got to. Where is she?'

" 'Listen, George. Elsie has no intention of going through any more unhappy years. The children are well adjusted in school, and Elsie's work pays reasonably well. She left a letter here for you. I'll mail it to you.'

" 'No, read it to me,' I said. 'Read it now, please.'

" 'Okay,' he said doubtfully. 'Hold the line until I go get it.' I heard his footsteps as he walked away from the telephone, and heard them returning. He read:

"George, darling, please, please don't try to find us. I've prayed so often, and with so many tears, that I know God will bring us all together again in His own good time. We love you, miss you, want you, need you, and pray for you. Be patient, my darling, and let God work things out for us. Someday . . .

"I tried to speak, but words wouldn't come. Her father said, 'You still there, George? You all right?'

" 'I'm all right,' I answered, and hung up the receiver.

"I'd been back in our home for less than a week when an acquaintance I'd stopped to talk with on the street said:

" 'By the way, George, I ate dinner last Saturday in your wife's restaurant in Salinas. Your daughter waited on me. Your boy was washing dishes. Good kids.'

" 'Well,' I said, 'if Elsie cooked your meal, it was a good one.'

" 'Yes, it was a good one,' he said. He looked as if he wanted to ask questions, so I went on nonchalantly:

" 'The restaurant was a temporary deal just to tide them over while I was in the hospital. They're going to close it out soon, and come home.'

"He walked on, but I stood where I was, mind in turmoil. My first impulse was to take a bus to Salinas at once, walk in on my family and gather them all in my arms. Once, I'd have done that. But now I remembered Father Ferraris' words: 'a mature man thinks of others, first.' I tried to put myself in Elsie's place. I'd no doubt she was living in dread that I'd show up drunk—spoil all that she and the children had accomplished the past two years. I imagined her nervousness whenever the telephone rang—her quick glance at each customer, to be sure it wasn't her tippling husband. I wanted to assure her that her fears were now groundless, but also realized that it'd require more than words to convince her that the years of misery and humiliation had ended. I walked on, thoughtfully.

"The odor of stale beer wafted from a tavern as I passed by. I licked my lips. In the next block I passed another. Again the odor of spirits. I paused, and sniffed. Loneliness flooded me. A few moments before, the things I'd wanted most were my wife and my children. Now the thing I wanted most was a drink. Inward struggle continued while I walked two more blocks.

"At the third block, with a groan, I walked into a bar. A juke box played softly. The bartender said, 'Yes, sir?'

"I clutched the bar's edge to still the trembling of my hands.

" 'Wait,' I said. 'Give me a minute.'

"The bartender picked up a glass, wiped it with a towel and said, 'Sure. Take your time.'

" 'Oh, God!' I cried softly, and tried to remember Elsie's face. It wouldn't come clear. The bartender said:

" 'You're sweating, Mister. It's cool in here. What's the matter? You sick?'

"I said hoarsely: 'God's here.'

" 'Huh?'

" 'I don't want to drink in front of God,' I said, and with shaking legs, walked toward the door. The bartender called after me, 'You really got 'em, brother.'

"A moment later I was blinking in the bright sunshine of the street.

"My battle'd been brief, but devastating. I was so weak that I feared I'd fall. It required all my will power to stay erect long enough to walk into a hotel and register for a room. I lay on the bed, eyes closed, filled with quiet happiness. With God's help, I'd won my battle. And I knew—with calm sureness—that I'd never need to go through it again. That was eight years ago," Moray said, "and I never have.

"I made no attempt to get in touch with Elsie, but continued to believe that all would be well with us again, as she'd said, 'in God's good time.' I was lonely living in the big house by myself, and for something to do evenings after I got home from my new office, I began working in Elsie's flower garden. She'd always loved her garden, and although I knew little about flowers, I began to find contentment there. The recent tenants had neglected the garden, so I tried to bring it back to former health and beauty. Before long, I was taking pride in what I'd accomplished with fertilizers, water and cultivation.

"One Saturday afternoon as I knelt beside a bed of Sweet William, the thought came to me that gardening was a form of prayer. Thereafter, as I worked, I prayed. I asked nothing for myself except God's continued guidance, but with all the urgency of a lonely heart, I asked God to protect and comfort my family. I began to look on each new bloom in Elsie's garden as assurance from God that He'd heard my prayers.

"One Sunday morning an old lawyer friend—an alcoholic whose drinking had taken him to prison—dropped in to say hello. He was moderately drunk, garrulous and bitter. Said he'd fought alcoholism until there was no fight left in him.

" 'It's a futile, hopeless struggle, George,' he said.

"I told him about Father Ferraris, and what he'd shown me about alcoholics. When I said I now believed that most drunkards were emotionally immature, my old friend was indignant.

" 'If *any* man's gained maturity the hard way,' he said testily, 'it's *I*. My life's been difficult, and increasingly unhappy. I've known hardship and disgrace. There's not one immature impulse left in me.'

"He and I had many talks thereafter, and little by little, he shed his antagonism toward himself, toward Man and toward God. Came the day long later, when he admitted that he, too, recognized that his drinking resulted from childish reactions and impulses. When a man sees himself as he really is, prayer becomes as natural as breathing. Prayer sustained my friend, and eventually he drank no more. I wish I could tell you his name—for today his reputation as a legal authority is known from coast to coast.

"During the past eight years, more than forty alcoholics—some completely down and out—have come my way for a time, and gone on—cured with God's help.

"That's about all there is to my story except that six months after I'd come home, and my practice appeared to be on the road to success, I left the office early one afternoon, came home and began puttering in the garden. As I knelt, working my fingers into the soil beside an ailing aster, I heard footsteps on the graveled walk behind me. I knew, instantly, that they were Elsie's. I didn't look up—just knelt, fingers suddenly motionless in the soil. She knelt beside me, then clutched my hand—held it to her breast.

" 'You'll get your blouse dirty, Elsie—my hands . . .'

" 'Darling!' she said.

"I held her close, and tried not to cry.

" 'You're home!' I said.

" 'Yes, George—home.' "

A PROFESSOR at Capetown (South Africa) University once told his class that everything that existed was a divine miracle.

A student sniggered.

"Don't you believe in miracles?" the professor asked him.

"No."

"You, that is to say—Man—is God's greatest miracle. Don't you believe in yourself?"

"I do," the student replied, "but not in the sense you mean."

"Will you tell us, please," the professor said kindly, "how red corpuscles are manufactured in our bone marrow? Or the astonishing story of how white corpuscles mobilize by the millons to attack infection? Or why it is that no man, by will power alone, can stop breathing sufficiently long to destroy himself? Explain, if you will, the millions of electrical connections that must be made within the brain just to recall a single memory. Or, perhaps you will tell us how the pictures seen by the eye are transformed into pictures in the mind. Tell us . . ."

"Sorry, sir," the student interrupted, "but I know practically nothing about the workings of the human body."

"Then," said the professor, "you will do well to study your body, for you cannot understand even one phase of its workings without believing in God. Learn even a little about yourself, my lad, and you'll believe in miracles."

He Prayed for a Miracle

WHEN I WENT to interview Curt Langford, a Campbell, California, road contractor, I found him in an inviting bungalow-type home. The large green lawn with its pink-flowering apricot trees, the banks of bright flowers under the windows, the proud rows of vegetables in the back garden all spoke of prosperity. The warm light in his wife's eyes and the exhilarating laughter of three small children as they played at being cowboys told, far better than words, that happiness dwelt among the Langfords.

Such had not been the case twelve months before. Then, Langford had had stomach ulcers, an erratic heart, a short temper, worry and fear. He'd had lots of work, but people were not paying their bills. There'd been new equipment to buy, old equipment to maintain, payrolls to meet. Langford had had no financial reserves.

As we sat on the wide porch, overhung by a branch of an orange tree just bursting into fragrant bloom, Langford said:

"A year ago I felt as if I were being sucked down into quicksand. The more I struggled to escape, the deeper I seemed to sink. And I couldn't stop struggling.

"Sometimes I thought of praying. But in school days, I'd concluded that God was a myth, that prayer was a refuge of the weak and timid.

"Today I can understand an ignorant, conceited kid holding such ideas, but for a man to continue to hold them until he's thirty-five years old . . .

"Anyway," he went on, *"now* I know that often only a cry of despair from a tortured soul is a prayer—a prayer to the God that a man's soul knows, but that his shuttered mind may not acknowledge. It was that kind of a prayer that brought me the lily bulbs."

"Bulbs?"

"Yes, twenty-four Easter lily bulbs." He pointed to dark-green lily plants growing beneath a shadowed window. "A neighbor of ours named Nolan, a floriculturist, sent them to me as a present. I didn't know anything about lilies. Those bulbs annoyed me. Anyway, my mind was on my troubles, and I didn't feel like gardening. But I knew Nolan would be asking about them, so one day I stopped at his home to ask for planting instructions.

"When we shook hands, Nolan asked, 'How's business?'

" 'Pretty bad,' I answered. 'Collections, particularly.'

" 'Oh well,' he said, smiling, 'prayer will fix that.'

" 'Prayer won't do me any good. My business is so far gone that only a miracle would save it.'

" 'Well, pray for a miracle,' Nolan said.

" 'You know as well as I do,' I answered, 'that there are no miracles these days—if there ever were any.'

"Nolan looked at me strangely. 'Well, well,' he said, motioning me into his house. 'Come in for a few minutes.' He seated me in a large, comfortable chair, then walked to the window and stared out across the lawn. I got the odd idea that he was praying silently.

"It made me uncomfortable. I said, 'About those lily bulbs. How deep do I plant them?'

" 'Ah yes, the lily bulbs,' he said. 'Curt, what do you know about chemistry?'

" 'Not much.'

" 'There's a series of complicated chemical reactions,' he said, 'that the best-equipped chemistry laboratory would require months to complete. Suppose I told you that I know a small factory that has so perfected the necessary processes that it accomplishes the entire chain of reactions in just about three seconds.'

"I knew Nolan was a great hand for investing in unusual enterprises, so assumed he was talking about one of them. 'Sounds good,' I said. 'What products result?'

" 'Oh, carbon water [carbohydrates], sugars, starches, and what not. But that's not the point. Those chemical reactions are so complicated that it'd require a book of five hundred pages to describe them, even briefly. This factory completes them—all of them—in only three seconds. Would you call that a miracle?'

" 'I guess I would,' I said.

" 'What's more, Curt, that carbon water, those sugars and starches are so necessary that if this little factory, and others like it, were not manufacturing them, *there would be no life on this earth.*'

" 'Well, Mr. Nolan, I'm not up to date on those things,' I said. 'I . . .' A memory stirred in my mind of something I'd once read. I said: 'Plants. You're talking about lily plants, I'll bet.'

" 'Yes—all plants. Their leaves are the factories.'

" 'Plants!' I said, irritated. 'I've got too much on my mind to stay here talking about plants.' I stood up. 'You stick plants in the ground, pour some water on their roots and they grow.'

" 'Now, Curt, stop acting as if you've no brain. Sit down!'

"I sat.

" 'Ground,' Nolan said. 'You mentioned ground. Soil. You seem to think that soil's only a dead mass. But soil is alive. It carries on all the functions of living things. It's composed of minute particles, and every particle contains minerals and chemicals locked within it. The minerals and chemicals are freed only when the soil particle is encased in a film of water. That water makes a minute electric battery of the soil particle, and ions are released to become food for plants. Some ions are exchanged with those of other soil particles, altering the acidity of the soil to one more suitable for plant growth. Humus in the soil is broken down into plant food by bacteria. These plant foods—about thirty-six different kinds—are absolutely essential to plant growth. Without water, they cannot be made available.

" 'Water!' He pointed to a large willow tree in his yard. 'Another miracle. From the soil, a steady column of water, impregnated with minerals and chemicals, is being forced up through the roots into the three hundred thousand leaves of that tree. Those minerals and chemicals cannot be used by the tree in their present forms, so the leaves filter them from the water, change them into sugars and starches, start them on a journey to billions of cells throughout that tree. Then the leaves spray the water through their pores into the air in an invisible mist—*two and one-half tons* of water from a large tree—*in one warm day.*

" 'That mist sprayed into the air from the leaves of grasses, weeds, shrubs, the trees—is part of God's great wheel—His wheel of living water. God's wheel, which has been revolving since the beginning of time—which will continue to revolve until the earth is no more! First mist, then clouds, then rain, falling upon a thirsty land. Water releasing chemicals and minerals from soil particles, so that the plants may grow and thrive and mature to help men grow and thrive and do His will. Again, mist, clouds and rainfall. Water—the water of life.

" 'You say, Curt, "You just pour water on the roots, and the plants grow." True, But why? Because all things—the plants, the soil, the water, the sunlight—are obeying a law— the law of God.'

" 'But business . . .' I began.

" 'Yes, business. Listen, my boy. There's nothing on the face of the earth that's not subject to God's law. Your business is on the rocks because you're violating that law. Where famine, floods and pestilence stalk, man has interfered with, or ignored, God's law for soil and plant life and water. Business firms go broke because God's law of business is violated.'

"Slowly and deliberately, Nolan went on: 'Everything is a miracle. Hand me some things out of your pockets, Curt.'

"I handed him a match, a rubber band, a small bottle of vitamin pills. He said: 'This match is wood. It's composed of atoms combined into molecules. Drop the match in water. It swells in circumference, but not in length. Wood molecules will not stretch lengthwise.

" 'This elastic band is also composed of atoms combined into molecules. The rubber band can be stretched in all directions, and returns to its original state when tension is relaxed. Dropped in water, it does not swell.

" 'Yet the only real difference between the two is the *arrangement* of the atoms. This arrangement of atoms is the chief difference in all forms of matter. Change one atom in anything, and you create something else.

" 'I see these vitamins are Vitamin D. Another miracle. A child stunted by a diet lacking in vitamins can be restored to normal growth by just enough Vitamin D to cover the point of a pin—and if the child thereafter receives a vitamin-sufficient diet, no more treatment will be required.

" 'Now, Curt, in the face of these marvelous testimonies to God's laws, do you still feel that He'll have any difficulty in helping you to solve your business problems?'

" 'No, I guess not,' I said. 'But what's God's law for busi ness?'

" 'Ask Him, Curt. He'll show you,' Nolan said.

"I went home and prayed—my first true prayer since boyhood.

"The next five weeks were strange and wonderful ones," Curt said, after a pause. "All my life I'd seen the trees, the grass, the birds, the flowers, the clouds, the rain, the sunshine and the shadows, but they'd been like paintings in a diorama. Static—just pictures. Then, day by day, a new world unfolded to me—a world of miracles. I began to sense the teeming life within the soil, and the wonderful activities of the leaf factories. I heard the song of water healing thirsty ground, heard the hymn of growing things. I felt the rhythm of the universe operating within God's law; saw that all was beauty, love, strength, harmony and obedience.

"Two firms owed me a lot of money. Neither had responded to my frequent, urgent requests for payment. I prayed about those bills. The answer came next morning as I wakened, but at the time, I didn't recognize it as an answer. It was an idea, an impulse—and it seemed fantastic to me. I pushed it out of my mind, but it kept recurring. I finally went to see Nolan.

" 'I've prayed about collections, Mr. Nolan,' I said, 'but nothing's happened except that I've developed a compulsion to do something that seems sort of foolish.'

" 'So?'

" 'For days,' I said, 'I've had a growing impulse to write my two chief debtors, saying: "I assume you're in bad financial straits; otherwise, you'd have paid what you owe me. You probably have all the worries you can bear, and I don't want to add to them. I'm enclosing your bill, marked *Paid in Full*. If you're really in need, please consider your bill now paid." '

"Nolan smiled. 'Go ahead with it, Curt,' he said. 'I'm curious to see what'll happen.'

"Well, I mailed those letters—and both firms paid."

Langford was thoughtful for a few moments. Then he said:

"When we ask something of God, we always get an answer. But God will answer in His own way—not ours. Sometimes the answers don't come immediately. A year ago, that answer to my heart's cry took a little time, for I had to be taught. First, the gift of lily bulbs that took me to a man whose words helped reveal the miracle of things that grow—then led me into the sunlight of faith." He paused. "Well, I guess you understand," he said.

"Yes," I said, "I understand."

*W*HILE *visiting near Missoula, Montana, in 1943, I met a devout but uncultured cowboy, Buckskin Pete Ferris, who'd experienced many remarkable answers to prayer. When I asked him if he used any particular form of prayer, he said:*

"I ask God to steer me right in whatever I'm about to do. That's all, except that I never forget to thank Him for all He's done for me."

"And your prayers are answered?" I asked.

"Always," he said.

"Are there types of prayers that are not answered?"

"Sure," he said. "God don't want to be asked to be a horse-trader, and He don't want to be asked to get out and 'root for Yale,' and He don't like to be dickered with. He don't answer such prayers."

"Horse-trader?"

"Well, some folks try to make a trade with God. They say: 'If You'll do this for me, God, then I'll do that for You.' Horse-trading, I call it."

"Root for Yale?"

"Well, there's people who ask God to take sides with them against other people. Like one time I heard a man pray that God would 'get out and root for Yale' in a football game. This man was a sort of evangelist. I heard him say in a meeting: 'If we pray hard enough, there's no reason why God won't get in there and pitch passes for Yale.' Seems to me that that sort of praying is an insult to God. Reckon God does, too, because the other team walloped Yale that game."

"Do you grow impatient when answers are delayed?" I asked.

"Rivers don't run to the sea all in a lump," Buckskin said. "Rain falls sort of slow and easy. Sunlight, they say, takes time to reach the Earth. There's lightning, of course, and lightning's mighty fast. Some answers to prayer come like that. Right now! But it don't lightning every day. No, I don't fret if answers don't come rushing up in a cloud of dust. I just know they'll get here—and there ain't no 'if' about that!"

Forget That "If"

BEGINNING WITH A shaving cream he developed while attending high school, chemist Antone Pannutti, president of Panco Manufacturing Company of Santa Clara, California, has built up a line of forty-three cosmetic products which he advertises as the most unusual in America.

Pannutti's products do not get moldy, do not turn rancid, do not harden or shrink or separate in the containers, do not become ropy, and are not harmed by heat or cold. If the tops of tubes and jars are left off for months, the contents remain soft and fragrant.

Behind this achievement are eleven years of research, an investment of $150,000 and a long series of answers to prayers . . . for Pannutti, inventor of more than three hundred items besides cosmetics, is a praying man.

As we sat in the sunny office of his modern factory, Pannutti said: "You see what I have here. Well, every brick in the building, every piece of equipment, every formula, has resulted from prayer. When I began developing my cosmetic line, I had neither the money nor the experience necessary to develop as I've done. When I realized this, there was only one thing for me to do: ask God to help me. He has.

"For you to understand how much He has helped me, I must start my story back there in my last year as a chemistry student at Georgetown University. I'd already determined to get into the cosmetic manufacturing business.

117

"One day I visited a drug wholesaler, and somehow got to telling him about my ambition. He said, 'Don't do it. Stay out of the cosmetic business; competition's too keen, and to put over a new line in America would require at least a half million dollars. There are better and easier fields for a young chemist.'

" 'I'm not afraid of competition if I can create a top quality line,' I answered. 'I'm young, and . . .'

" 'Too young! Look,' he said, shaking a finger at me, 'cosmetics and perfumes are one of our big headaches. They deteriorate on druggists' shelves. Last year we had to take back more than $55,000 worth of spoiled cosmetics from our retailers. No, my boy, get into something else.'

" 'Cosmetics that won't deteriorate can be created,' I said.

" 'Do you think you can stop face creams from turning rancid?' he asked. 'Can you keep lotions and pastes from getting moldy? Can you figure out some way to prevent creams from hardening when women leave the jar tops off?'

" 'Sure I can,' I said. 'Why not?'

"He smiled skeptically. 'Better men than you have tried it, and failed. The job's too big.'

"Well, that remark got my dander up," Pannutti went on. "I was determined to succeed where other chemists had failed. Before long, however, I realized that the wholesaler had been right—the job was too big for me—alone. I needed God's help. Prayer was the answer.

"My mother had taught me about prayer. Some of my boyhood escapades would have had serious consequences had my mother not known how to pray. She's a fine, old-country Italian with an abiding love of God in her heart. She used to tell me: 'God will never fail you. If you sometimes think He has, you can be sure, my son, that it is you who have failed Him. Work hard, work honestly, aim high, live clean, and be thankful to God for all He has given you. And in your time of need, God will support you.'

"When I set out to create new cosmetic formulas, my greatest need was for money. I prayed. One night I wakened from sleep with an idea for a dry-cleaners' spotting pencil—one that would quickly take out almost any type of stain. I went into my little lab, mixed up the ingredients, tried out the pencil—and it worked. I sold the formula for enough money to buy laboratory equipment, chemicals and ingredients for my first cosmetic experiments.

"A few months later, I was out of cash again. The experiments stopped. I went to my mother. We prayed together. She said: 'Now rest easy, Son. Don't be impatient. The answer will come.'

"It did come. I had trouble with a zipper one morning, and as I fussed with it, saw a way to improve it. I patented the idea, and sold the patent for $5,000. With that money, I enlarged my lab, laid in a stock of chemicals, bought an incubator and a refrigerator, and began work on the prevention of molds.

"I'd mix a formula, put part of it in the incubator, and part in the refrigerator. I wanted products that would stand up in both cold and heat. In time, I developed a formula that would not deteriorate in the refrigerator, but molds continued to develop in the incubator.

"Nineteen months of earnest work went by. One morning I took my four-hundred-and-forty-third formula from the incubator. It was moldy—and I was again out of money. I locked up my lab and went home, discouraged. My wife stood my moping uncomplainingly as long as she could, then said, 'You've been overworking. Let's go on a vacation.'

" 'What with?' I wanted to know. 'I'm out of money again.'

" 'Have you prayed?' she asked.

" 'No,' I said, 'I haven't prayed. All I've ever done is to ask God to help me. He must be getting tired of it.'

" 'Now you're acting childish,' my wife said. 'You know perfectly well that God wants to help you. He always has— and He always will.'

"I guess I was tired out, all right, for I broke down and cried. I'm one of those Italians who cry or laugh easily, anyway. After a while, I knelt and asked God to forgive me for my recent attitude. I remember saying: 'God, you made the laws of chemistry; please show me how to prevent those molds.'

"While I was still on my knees, the answer came: *the preventative of the molds was within the molds.* The revelation sent me rushing back to my lab. I worked straight through for forty-eight hours, breaking down the molds. I finally got a gray powder, with which I inoculated a batch of face cream. I put some of the cream in the incubator, and some of it up on the hot roof. I left the lab, borrowed a little money and took my wife on a two-week vacation.

"I returned to the lab certain that God had answered my prayer. He had. There was no mold on the cream in the incubator.

"I went to the roof, inspected the cream that had been undergoing the heat of summer suns, and the chill of night. No mold.

"God had helped me to make what I believe is a great discovery. The United States Army is now testing my formula as a possible cure for jungle rot— a disease that affects the skin.

"With the most difficult phase of my research over, I needed a factory. I set about perfecting some inventions that had been in the back of my mind for a long time. With God's help, I developed some basic patents on radio-controlled airplanes; a new type of miniature radio; a new type of detergent; a new method of applying fertilizer; and numerous minor improvements on existing patents.

"In five years, those inventions brought me a little more than $150,000. Of course, all that time I was also working on my cosmetic line."

Pannutti waved his arm in a comprehensive arc. "I bought this building," he said. "I bought all that equipment out there. This is a good building, fireproof and explosion-proof. I have a growing demand for my products right here in California. I ship some to Italy, and some to South America. Ours will be a nationally-sold product in God's own time."

"You're making money?" I asked.

Pannutti laughed. "Just about breaking even," he said, "but not quite. Truth is, two creditors are pressing me hard right now. I could borrow some more, of course, but I don't feel that God wants me to do that. I owe these two creditors about $2,500—not a great deal, but they're making such a fuss that it's causing dissension among my stockholders. I've prayed about it."

As I got up to go, I said, "Mr. Pannutti, will you let me know if and when and how you get the $2,500?"

"Sure," he said, "but forget that 'if' "

On July 16, 1951, my telephone rang. It was Pannutti. "I got that money," he said, "you know, that $2,500."

"I was sure you would," I said. "Another invention, I suppose."

Pannutti laughed. "I could never invent anything so astonishing as the answer to that prayer of mine for the $2,500. Listen:

"Night before last, my wife heard a knock on the door. She went to the door and opened it. No one was there. A few minutes later, another knock came. This time, I went to answer. Again no one was there. I thought maybe some youngsters were playing tricks. I unlatched the screen door and pushed it open. A white envelope lay on the porch. I picked it up, and as I did so, I heard a car across the street start off into the night.

"I opened the envelope. Inside was $2,500 in currency, and a short note. The note read:

"You can repay this some day when I let you know who I am. Early tonight I was sitting in a restaurant booth, and heard two men boasting of how they were going to get their fingers into your business because of a $2,500 debt you owe. Their attitude annoyed me. I felt I had to spoil their game. Please pay those creditors off at once. You'll hear from me later.

"No name on the note?" I asked.

"No name," Pannutti said.

I was slow in commenting on the story, so Pannutti said: "Well? Do you find it hard to believe?"

"No," I said, "I'm only wondering how I can write your story and make the world believe it."

"That's easy," Pannutti answered. "Just send it out with a prayer."

S HORTLY after Duncan Moffit, of "God's Jelly Bean Road," became well enough to work the prospect shaft he'd sunk on the bank of the Goat River, the shaft became hopelessly flooded. Moffit was dismayed, for pumping equipment was out of his financial reach. His wife, Ruby, however, whose prayers had helped sustain him through a long period of hardship, said to him:

"Perhaps the shaft was sunk in the wrong place, Duncan. Perhaps God permitted the shaft to flood. That might be His way of telling us that the galena vein you're searching for is somewhere else."

Moffit couldn't immediately accept this idea of Ruby's. He prayed about it.

A few days later, while half-heartedly swinging a pick at the edge of his claim, it drove deep into galena ore. He shoveled away a shallow covering of earth, traced the vein to the river's edge, crossed the river, picked the vein up on the opposite shore, and there he staked another claim.

Later, for a comfortable sum, Moffit sold his claims to the Leadville Mining Company.

God's Jelly Bean Road

SOME OF DUNCAN Moffit's fear of the future lifted as he paused in the approaching dusk, at the edge of a snow-filled clearing in southeastern British Columbia, and saw the little three-room log cabin snuggling close to the pine trees less than fifty paces away.

"Home again!" he said softly.

To ease the pain of the war-wound in his back, he leaned against the ice-crusted trunk of a spruce tree. He was very tired. The six-mile walk from the railroad junction through woods white with knee-deep snow had taken eight hours—almost too sustained an effort for a man newly out of an army hospital. He knew he should have stayed overnight at the junction, and hired Indian George next morning to break trail for him. But for three years of war, his arms had ached to hold close to him his wife and his two little girls.

Doggedly, during those eight hours, he'd plodded on, pushing snow aside with his shins. There'd been no wind among the trees, and his heavy army uniform had grown damp with sweat. When his back had pained too much, he'd lain against a drift—but not for long, for chill comes quickly. Every tree, every white-capped rock along the trail had been familiar. He'd traveled that way often when he and Ruby were building the cabin; clearing patches for vegetables and flowers; doing assessment work on their silver-lead mining claim.

As he thought of the claim, a sickness swept through him, for the claim had been his hope of financial security. That he'd have to muck, and shovel, and drill alone, perhaps for years, had not bothered him then, for he'd delighted in his strength.

Now as he leaned against the spruce he thought of the many months ahead while he'd wait for health to return—the claim going unworked. The old dream of happiness seemed dim.

Some years later, when I asked Moffit to tell his story, he said, "I'll write it for you." Here it is:

"Those moments beside the spruce tree were a low spot in my life. And then I pretended that Ruby, soft-voiced and courageous, stood beside me, holding my hand as she'd done many past times when, weary of work, we'd strolled in the forest for quiet and peace.

"The youngsters, Rhoda and Essie, had been about three and two years old when I went to war. Now Rhoda was six, and Essie, five. They'd be changed; they'd be taller—yet I knew the mischievous twinkle would still be in Rhoda's dark eyes; the calm, steady sweetness would still be in Essie's gray ones.

"Dusk deepened as I loitered. Suddenly the kitchen window glowed golden as a lighted oil lamp was put on the table. Light streamed outward over the snow, making a welcoming pathway for my feet—and my feet were now eager. The door creaked as I opened it. Ruby turned from the kitchen stove, saw me, and her hand went to her heart. The next instant she was in my arms, and the hands of my two little girls were pulling at me, voices shrilling, 'Daddy! Daddy! Daddy!'

"Something cooking on the stove boiled over, and Ruby ran to rescue it. The girls pushed me into an old platform-rocker, then each climbed on a knee. Essie said:

" 'Now we can have the party.'

" 'What party?' I asked.

"Rhoda laughed. 'Don't pretend, Daddy. Your coming-home party, of course.'

" 'Oh, sure,' I grinned. 'I brought something for the party in my pack, but the pack was too heavy, so I left it at the junction. Indian George, or one of the trappers will bring it next time they come out this way.'

" 'Is it a secret—that's in the pack?' Essie asked.

"I hugged both girls close. 'No secrets,' I said, 'It's some jelly beans and chocolate bars, and . . .

" 'The dollhouse!' Rhoda offered happily.

"I looked at Ruby. 'I promised them a dollhouse when you got home; a little one,' she said. 'There's no hurry.'

" 'Is it in the pack, Daddy?' Essie's eyes were solemn.

" 'Don't worry, Baby,' I said, 'you'll have your dollhouse.'

" 'Supper,' Ruby announced as she carried steaming bowls to the table.

"We took our places. From the center of the red-and-white checked cloth, lamplight encircled us with cozy warmth. The old copper teakettle on the range began to sing. Ruby looked at me and said: 'Oh, Duncan—you're home!'

"We bowed our heads for grace.

"After the old-fashioned oatmeal porridge had been eaten to the last drop of sugared milk, Ruby brought hot scones from the oven, then poured tea for herself and me. As she poured milk for the girls, Rhoda said, 'Daddy's a special occasion, isn't he, Mama?'

" 'Very special,' Ruby smiled. She went to a cupboard and returned with a small bottle of red vegetable coloring. She poured a few drops in each glass of milk. The girls stirred, and the milk turned pink.

" 'We drink pink milk, Daddy,' Rhoda said, 'only with the most important people.'

"After the children, in long, flowered-flannel nightgowns, had been tucked into bed, I said to Ruby:

" 'We must face it, darling. Even if I were well enough to work the claim, we'd not be able to get the ore to the smelter unless we build a road to the junction. A road would cost about $15,000. The Lang family's working five claims at Seven-mile, and they'll need to start shipping ore soon. If the Langs would come in on the road for five shares, then our share—for one claim—would be about $2,500. But we need other things, too—a forge, dynamite, new drills, hammers— say another $600. We'd need about $3,100 for everything.'

" 'I have sixteen dollars, dear,' Ruby said.

" 'And I've nine dollars. My pension will be about thirty-five dollars a month. It's a hopeless situation, Ruby. We'll be lucky to eat!'

" 'Duncan,' Ruby said, 'the root cellar's still half-full of potatoes, turnips, carrots and squash. We've lots of wild berries I canned last summer. The cow's been fresh for only two months. We've really very little to worry about. You can rest a lot, and get strong again.'

" 'I'm tired, Ruby,—and frightened,' I said. 'I think we should try to sell the claim—even if we can't get what we've put into it.'

" 'Oh, Duncan, we mustn't sell now, after all the years of work, and the sacrifices we've made to keep it.' Ruby walked to the window and looked into the night. After a moment she said: 'The moon's up, Duncan. Let's go outside.'

"She put a plaid shawl around her shoulders, took my hand and led me into the moonlight. The air was quiet, but branches of dark trees sighed and creaked under burdens of snow. The stars shone jewel-bright. Ruby lifted her face.

" 'Those wonderful stars,' she said.

" 'Ruby,' I said, 'let's be practical. I'm whipped. The only hope for us is for me to go to Winnipeg and get a job I can handle. I'll try to save enough money to send for you and the girls. There's no use hanging onto shattered dreams. We'll give up this place, and . . .'

" 'We see God's stars every night,' Ruby said, as if she hadn't heard what I'd said. 'Suppose we were never to see them again!' She turned and took both my hands. 'The trees,' she said. 'Remember, Duncan, what you quoted about the trees that first night we were here—seven years ago?'

" 'That the groves were God's first temples,' I said.

" 'Yes. And remember what else you said that night?'

" 'Yes. I said I felt nearer to God here than I'd ever felt anywhere else—that I thought this must be the place He wanted us to have our home.'

" 'How can you be afraid of the future, Duncan, here in one of God's groves, under His stars?'

" 'But . . .'

"She held me close, then said: 'Let's say a prayer, right here, now, Duncan.' Together, we knelt in the snow.

" 'Dear God,' Ruby said, 'please show us how to build the road, and keep us unafraid.'

"Five days later, when Indian George brought my pack, I found the chocolate bars squashed, but the jelly beans were unhurt. That night after the girls were asleep, I cut five bean-shaped holes in each of several four-inch-square pasteboard cards.

" 'Did you know,' I asked Ruby, 'that the body of a pig is shaped like a bean? Watch.' Around each hole I drew a pig's legs, tail and head. Then I pushed jelly beans into the holes. Ruby smiled:

" 'What darling little porkers, Duncan! The girls will love them.'

"I picked up a card, pushed a red jelly bean into one hole, a yellow bean into another, a black bean, a purple bean, and a green bean. The colorful little pigs looked so cheerful that I couldn't resist waking the girls to show them my invention. They were delighted, and spent at least twenty minutes pushing different colored beans into holes, exclaiming over the effects. They ate only the less attractive, or misshapen jelly beans, and fell asleep at last with bean-filled cards all over the quilt.

"I made the dollhouse from a tin export soda-cracker box, and painted doors and windows on it with Rhoda's watercolors. I cut out a small door, and hinged it with loops of wire. Then I painted shingles on the roof, and was busy painting flowers and vines on the walls when Ruby said, 'It's two o'clock in the morning, Duncan. The dollhouse is beautiful, but you've done enough. Tomorrow's the day of the party, remember.'

"The next afternoon, in the middle of the party, a stranger knocked on the door. 'I heard you were home again, Mr. Moffit,' he said. 'I'm Jack Lang. We're getting quite a dump of ore at our mine, and we'll have to build that road to the junction. Thought you ought to join us. Your share of the cost will be about $2,500.'

" 'I'll have to think about it, Mr. Lang,' I said. 'Won't you come in and get warm? We're having a party.'

"Lang joined us, and patted Essie's shoulder. Essie said, 'Look! We can make purple pigs, or green pigs, or red pigs, or pink pigs, or any color pigs!' She pushed jelly beans out of a card, held the card toward Lang and said, 'You can change the colors!'

"Lang took the card, pushed jelly beans in and out of holes, his face thoughtful. 'Not a bad idea for the penny trade,' he said. 'I'm sales manager for a candy manufacturing company, you know.'

"Rhoda said: 'Daddy made them all by himself. Our Daddy's the smartest man in the world.'

"Lang grinned. 'Well, anyway,' he said as he rose to leave, 'I think your Daddy had a smart idea about these pigs.'

" 'I'll let you know about my share in the road in a few days,' I said, and felt guilty about stalling, knowing $2,500 was out of the question.

"For several days after Lang's visit, I brooded. One evening after the girls had gone to bed, I burst out bitterly, 'We'll never have any money while I sit here like a knot on a log. We've been kidding ourselves about things, Ruby. We'll have to sell the claim.'

" 'But, darling, be patient,' Ruby said. 'God will . . .'

" 'God,' I said too loudly, 'has gone to the city—to Winnipeg—anywhere where I can earn money. I'm sick, and worried, and useless. I . . .' I stopped as muffled sobbing came from the bedroom.

"Ruby went in and came back with Essie in her arms. Essie held out her arms to me. I took her and she clung to me, weeping.

" 'Baby, Baby,' I said. 'Tell Daddy.'

" 'God's gone away!' Essie wailed. 'You said it, Daddy. God's gone to Winnipeg. He doesn't love us any more.'

" 'Darling,' I said, 'listen to Daddy. God's still here, just as He's always been. God's everywhere. Daddy didn't mean God wasn't here. I only meant . . .' I looked at Ruby helplessly.

" 'God's here, Essie,' Ruby said, 'right here in our house—in our hearts. He'll never leave us, Essie. He's right here close, protecting and loving us.'

"Essie sighed. 'I guess I just had a bad dream, Daddy,' she said. 'God didn't go away.'

" 'It was Daddy who had the bad dream, dear,' Ruby said.

"After Ruby took Essie back to bed, I got down on my knees beside the rocking chair. I must have prayed with rare concentration, for when I arose, the lamp was turned low, and Ruby had gone to bed.

"Three weeks later, Indian George brought me a letter from the Pacific Coast Biscuit Company, of Seattle. It said:

> . . . *and we have considered the jelly bean card idea submitted to us by Mr. Lang. For all rights to the idea, we offer you $3,600. If this is satisfactory, please let us know at once, and we will forward a release for you to sign. When we have received the signed release, we will immediately forward our check.*

"And so, the forest road that runs from Seven-mile to the junction, was built. Most people call it the Trail Road, but Ruby, Rhoda, Essie, and I, call it—God's Jelly Bean Road."

*J*OHN HABINE, *the man who trusted others for millions, died at the age of eighty-one. His will, after listing beneficiaries, ended with this quotation from Bishop Heber:*

> *We have a friend and protector, from whom, if we do not ourselves depart from Him, nor power nor spirit can separate us. In His strength let us proceed on our journey, through the storms, and troubles, and dangers of the world. However they may rage and swell, though the mountains shake at the tempests, our rock will not be moved: we have one friend who will never forsake us; one refuge, where we may rest in peace and stand in our lot at the end of the days.*

They Trusted Others
for Ten Million Dollars

WHEN I WAS A newspaper reporter I used to run across stories showing the power of prayer to help men achieve success and prosperity. One such story began:

"During the last twenty years, Paul Klein and John Habine, Canadian electrical contractors, have sold more than ten million dollars' worth of goods on credit—and have never lost a dime."

I didn't mention until the last paragraph that Klein and Habine owed their unusual financial record to prayer—but the story was killed on the city desk.

Going through some old files recently, I ran across my original notes about these two contractors.

I met Klein and Habine one August afternoon in San Diego where they were vacationing with their families. I'd been strolling through a park and had paused to watch four shirt-sleeved men pitching horseshoes. They were having so much fun that I sat on a nearby bench to watch. One of the four was fat, and when he heaved a horseshoe his stance was like something out of a comic book. Everyone laughed at him, and he laughed hardest.

I turned to a man seated on the bench beside me and said, "That's the jolliest fat man I've ever seen."

"That's Johnny," the man said fondly, "Johnny Habine, my business partner. He hasn't had a worry for twenty years."

"Rich?"

"No—Johnny's never saved much money. Gives most of it to the needy. Figures he's giving it back to God, who made it possible for him to earn it in the first place."

"I'm collecting stories about how God helps people," I said, "particularly, in everyday problems. Someday I'm going to put them all in a book. Tell me about Habine."

"Well," the man said, "my name is Klein—Paul Klein. Johnny and I grew up together. At seventeen we joined the same Canadian army outfit. That was in 1916. We went through two years of the war together, and we've been in business together ever since.

"We were discharged in Winnipeg, and took an army rehabilitation course in electricity. Although we had very little money, prayer made it possible for us to buy a little electrical shop.

"It was tough sledding for a while, and sometimes we were lucky to eat. Then one day a Dukhobor farmer ordered a farm light and power plant from us, gave us an order to wire his buildings, and paid cash. The firm of Klein and Habine was on its way.

"During the next two years we sold light and power plants to farmers all over Saskatchewan and Manitoba. Most farmers had little cash, but they gave us notes payable at harvest time. Harvest was good, and the notes were met promptly. Our bank account grew fat.

"But the third year was a drought year. Many notes were not met at harvest. We'd discounted them at the bank, and we had to make them good. It broke us.

"When we asked the banker for a loan to carry us along, he said, 'We can't gamble on another cropless year. But you lads aren't too bad off. You can recover most of your losses at law.'

"Johnny said: 'You mean we should sue?'

" 'Exactly.'

" 'But,' Johnny said, 'those farmers can't pay. They've lost their crops. If we got judgment on those notes, they'd have to sell everything they own.'

" 'That's the risk they took. There's no reason why you boys should stand the losses.'

"Johnny said: 'I don't think you understand. We want to help those people. They'll pay up when they get a crop. Before we installed those light plants, those farmers lived through the long winters by lamp and lantern light. Life's hard for them.'

"The banker turned away. 'Well, come and see me when you grow up,' he said.

"We stood on a street corner for a few minutes while Johnny cooled off. I said, 'Now we've done it.'

"Johnny was always a great one for laughing. He laughed then. He said: 'I'm going to the shop to pray. There's nothing to worry about, Paul.'

" 'We haven't prayed much lately,' I admitted.

" 'We got too cocky,' Johnny said. 'The banker was right in a way. It's time we grew up. Coming?'

"Well, three days later we got a phone call from one of our wholesalers asking us to come over to his office. When we were seated beside his desk, he began, 'I hear you boys told the banker you wouldn't sue the farmers for your money. Right?'

" 'Yes.'

" 'Why?'

"Johnny said: 'Well, what sense is there in selling people something to make their lives easier and happier, only to take it away again? A lawsuit would break most of those farmers, anyway. In some cases, it'd break their hearts, too.'

" 'Do you owe the bank any money?'

" 'No,' I told him, 'we made those notes good. But we're busted.'

" 'I was reared on a Saskatchewan wheat farm,' the wholesaler said. 'I remember my mother's hands in the winter—red, and chapped so deep that they bled. I can see them now as she struggled at the line to take off the clothes, frozen stiff as boards. I remember the bitter dark of winter mornings when I used a sledge to jar the runners of the horsedrawn bobsled loose from the frozen ground. I remember my father, his breath like steam, bucking wood for the kitchen stove by lantern light. I remember spring, and the horses and wagon slithering and sliding in the ankle-deep mud of the lane.

" 'Then plowing and planting and soon the bright green of the fields. The new wheat growing and with it, our hopes for harvest. Some years the hail came like charging horses, trampling and crushing, and in minutes our hopes were flattened and broken like the wheat. Other years we had the fiery sun, day after day, and the hot winds that burned and shriveled the wheat before our eyes. And when we knew for sure that the harvest was not to be—my mother's face, set and white, her arms hanging limp, and my father's eyes dark with hurt and discouragement.

" 'But the good years! My mother's quiet smile as she listened at the open door to the hum of my father's reaper. Those years I got books for Christmas, and shoes.' He paused, then went on, 'I'm glad you boys aren't going to sue anybody. I'm going to stake you for another year. I'm going to pick up those notes that you lads made good, and repay you in full.'

"Johnny said: 'Those farmers will all pay up some day.'

"The wholesaler smiled. 'I know they will,' he said. 'I'm a praying man too, you know.' Then he added: 'I've only one stipulation to make. After this, when a man's ready to buy a plant, tell him to mail you his notes *after he's prayed about the deal himself.'*

" 'But,' I said, 'we can't just order a man to pray! After all, if he wants a farm lighting plant . . .'

" 'Canada's a praying country,' the wholesaler said. 'Most of our great leaders, our engineers, our industrialists, our doctors, are praying men. So are the heads of many of our police departments. Think of the railroad contractor, Ian McKenzie. Do you think Lord Mount Stephen, Lord Strathcona, Sir William Van Horne, and the others could have built the Canadian Pacific Railroad without God's help? We're only nine million people, but we've turned vast prairies into fruitful fields; we've conquered mountains, rivers, forests. We're a great nation, and we're great because prayer made it possible.

" 'You boys in your small way, are part of God's plan for Canada. When you leave a farm lighted and powered, you've inaugurated a new era for that family. You bring a measure of the good things of life. Your installations are a reward to them for hard and faithful endeavor. Keep it up, lads, and go on with God's help. And let this be your motto: *Love worketh no ill to his neighbor.'* "

Habine ended his game and came over to sit beside us, wiping his face with his handkerchief. Klein introduced us, then went on:

"I'll admit that at first I was a little backward about asking men to pray over a deal they'd already decided they wanted. But, it worked. After praying, a few changed their minds, but about as many, who hadn't been sure that they wanted our plants, prayed, and decided they did want them. We had a big year.

"Canada's prairie provinces are dotted with small towns. Many of them are snowed-in all winter—sometimes from October to May. If we could bring a new era to the farms, why not to the towns? We tried it, and that year we sold nine-teen town plants. The towns issued bonds for the engines, generators and power lines. The merchants bought the bonds. Sometimes it took months to collect our money, but we were always paid.

"As we did with the farmers, we asked town councils to pray before signing up a deal. Some seemed a bit surprised. But none refused. That was twenty years ago. We've been busy ever since. Never got too big—just plugged along. We're not well educated and we're not smart. But we're working with God the best way we can. We've sold more than ten million dollars' worth of goods on credit since that whole-saler staked us, and we've never lost a penny."

"By trying to help our fellow men," Habine said, "we've helped ourselves, too."

"How about the wholesaler who staked you?" I asked.

"He never lost a penny either," Habine said. "It was his own money he used to take over those notes—not his com-pany's. Every delinquent farmer paid up. No one has ever lost money by dealings with Klein and Habine—because God is our senior partner."

He chuckled. "It's sure been fun," he said.

A BLIND organist once told me that the three things sighted persons do that aggravate him the most, are:

(a) Lead him across a street, then say "Wup! That's the curb!"—after he stumbles over it.

(b) Take him to a strange bedroom, show him his bed, then say: "You'll find the light switch by the door."

(c) Tell him where the looking-glass is located.

Blindcraft suggests these six "don'ts" in association with the blind:

1. DON'T treat blind persons as though they were abnormal specimens of humanity. Never talk to a blind man as though he were deaf, and do not imagine that the mere possession of sight implies superior knowledge.

2. DON'T refer to blindness as an "affliction"—it is a handicap. Never express sympathy for a blind person in his hearing, for you don't please him any more than you would please a cripple by discussing lameness in his presence; there are more practical outlets.

3. DON'T try to carry a blind person when he is entering a street car or train, crossing a road or going upstairs. He is not usually lame, and only needs to have his hand placed on a handle or rail. A touch on the arm is sufficient for leading. You need not help him sit down once he knows the position of his chair.

4. DON'T "tack" when piloting him across a road, go straight across if possible; otherwise you may upset his reckoning or cause him to side-stumble on reaching the curb. Sound and touch are the blind man's "sights," so do not push him before you in strange places. Go first, his hand touching you, that he may "see" where you are going.

5. *DON'T think that a blind guest is a serious responsibility, or that he will break up your home, or need someone to dress, bib and feed him!*

6. *DON'T address a blind man through an intermediary. For instance, don't ascertain if he takes sugar in his coffee by enquiring of his wife or friend; his own mentality is usually capable of enlightening you on any such matter.*

The Industry That Prayer Built

ONE MORNING IN 1914, Mark Bevin, a ships' chandler on San Francisco's Embarcadero, looked up from a jumble of ships' hardware to stare at a personable young woman who'd just entered through the street door. Bevin, rough but kindly, waited for her to speak. She said:

"I'm Ruth Quinan, Mr. Bevin, and I've come to ask you to teach me to splice rope."

"To splice rope, Lady?—you? Do you feel all right?" Bevin asked solicitously.

Ruth Quinan smiled, and explained, "I want to learn to splice rope so I can teach others to do it. You see, Mr. Bevin, I've taken a contract to splice *tons* of rope."

"*Tons* of rope! But your hands, Lady! I mean—even strong sailors find splicing a hard chore. Your hands are too small, and too weak."

"*My* hands may be weak," Ruth Quinan said, "but the hands of the blind are strong, and are eager to work."

"The blind? Look, Miss, suppose we go into my office and talk this over. Who's blind?"

Seated on a high stool at a bookkeeper's sloping desk, Ruth Quinan explained:

"Recently, Mr. Bevin, I was visiting a group of seven blind persons who have two rooms on California Street that they use as a workshop. Two men were weaving baskets, one was weaving a rug. Four girls, seated at a table, were sewing and making raffia baskets. A limousine stopped at the door, and a wealthy woman entered, followed by her chauffeur, carrying ice cream cones. They graciously passed around the cones, then left.

"One of the blind men was Albert Dickson, who wove baskets during the day to supplement earnings from playing his accordion in the streets, at night. For a while after the woman had gone, Dickson licked his cone thoughtfully, then said:

" 'If that lady's husband would give us jobs, we could earn wages and buy our own ice cream cones . . .' His voice trailed off.

"The undertone of frustration in Mr. Dickson's voice, Mr. Bevin, made me realize that the blackness of sightless eyes is not so deep as the blackness of spirit, caused by lack of opportunity to be self-supporting. I realized that the jobless blind are slaves—that work at fair wages sets them free.

"Something had to be done for these people, Mr. Bevin. When I got home that afternoon, I prayed about them.

"Until the revelation of the ice cream cones," Ruth Quinan went on, "I'd looked forward to a career in music. I'd worked long and hard toward that. But when I rose from my knees after praying that day, the rest of my life was dedicated to the blind.

"This splicing contract will give my people work. None of them has ever spliced rope; they must be taught. So, if you will teach me, I will teach them."

"I sure will, Miss Quinan," Bevin said. And Bevin did.

Thus was born Blindcraft, the department of *The California Association for the Blind* that makes it possible for the sightless to be self-supporting. During the forty years that Ruth Quinan was Blindcraft's president and business manager, thousands of blind found *freedom* in well-paid work, and the fame of their craftsmanship—particularly in woven furniture—has spread to far corners of the world. Blindcraft, begun in two shabby rooms on California Street, today is housed in a modern three-story building, and from its workshops comes a steady flow of brooms, rugs, baskets and furniture.

Says Eric W. Coster, editor of Blindcraft's magazine, *The California Beacon:*

"When Ruth A. Quinan heard and answered the plea of Albert Dickson, and other blind persons—for an opportunity to be men among men—she was soon to find that she'd not given up her musical career after all, but instead, had expanded its scope.

"The care of blind persons is a profession that demands the artistry, understanding and depth of feeling of the true musician, combined with quite inartistic hard work, and what Ruskin called 'an infinitude of tenderness, which is the chief gift and inheritance of great men'—and women.

"The success of Blindcraft in caring for every need of blind persons is due to the extraordinary degree to which Ruth Quinan possessed those qualities."

Quality of products is Blindcraft's pride. Workers tell of a wealthy man who ordered a second porch settee to match one he'd bought ten years before. The old settee was brought to the workshop so it could be duplicated. It was, of course, weathered and stained, but showed no other evidence of wear. Workers cleaned the old settee, and delivered it together with the new one. The two were placed side-by-side on their owner's porch. He examined them carefully, finally said, "Astonishing. I can't tell which is old, nor which is new."

Blindcraft's success did not come easy, nor did it come quickly. To the two rooms on California Street, Ruth Quin-

an added an upper flat to be used as office, library and cooking school. The flat and the lower rooms needed painting,
but there was no money to hire painters, so Ruth Quinan
took brush in hand and did the job herself. That same year,
the trademark, "Blindcraft," was adopted.

At first the products of the blind were marketed at semi-
annual sales in large department stores, and the returns di-
vided among the workers. In 1918 a vacant store on Stockton
Street was donated, and here, sales increased so materially
that a permanent location was acquired on Sutter Street. Increased sales made it necessary to get larger quarters for in-
dustrial activities, so the California Street property was sold,
and a three-story building on Folsom Street was leased.

There was no money to hire moving vans, so Blindcraft
was moved in two donated drays—Ruth Quinan driving one
of the two-horse teams. Incidentally, the driver of the other
dray later became blind, and worked at Blindcraft for many
years.

In 1923, fire destroyed the Folsom Street building, and
things looked black for Blindcraft. "But," Ruth Quinan explained, "none of us despaired. Instead, we prayed. God
heard us, and the Cowell family of San Francisco erected a
modern, three-story building on Howard Street, and deeded
it to *The San Francisco Association for the Blind*. That has
been our home ever since."

Before her death recently, Ruth Quinan told friends:

"Everything that Blindcraft has accomplished is the result
of prayer. Prayer has even changed the attitude of the public toward the blind. Not so long ago, a surprising number
of people treated blindness as something contagious. Today
almost everyone knows that blindness is not an affliction,
but a handicap—a handicap that can be largely overcome."

Ruth Quinan believed that "prayer points out the work,

and then we must dig in and do it." She was always at the Blindcraft factory at seven o'clock each morning to greet the first workers as they came on shift, then to check orders on hand, materials for the day, and deliveries to be made.

Then—when many executives are still lingering over breakfast—she went to her office in the salesroom, the nerve center of Blindcraft. Here she planned operations of the factory, activities of field secretaries, answered mail, and extended help and friendship to the blind in many ways.

"Yet," says Beverly Schultz, Blindcraft's business secretary, "in Ruth Quinan's office was no air of immediacy, no feeling of pressure. She gave no hint of her constant struggle to make one dollar do the work of two. The atmosphere of her office was one of peace, patience and prayer. 'The boss' was always calm and confident."

Often Ruth Quinan stayed in the office until late at night, doing paper work for which there had been no time during the day, and occasionally wielded a broom when the janitor had missed a day of work. Once when rats invaded the building, she sat up nights, keeping them out of the broomcorn.

Nothing seemed to faze "the boss." During one of San Francisco's Clean-up Day Parades, when there was no money to hire a band to lead blind marchers, Ruth Quinan got two large dishpans, and used them as drums—to the delight of San Franciscans.

Her prayers and example changed the attitude of much of the world toward the blind. Today in Hawaii, China, New Zealand, India, Switzerland, Australia, Egypt, England, and many other countries, friends and workers for the welfare of the blind turn more and more to Blindcraft, for advice.

Wrote Amal Shah, founder-secretary of the National Association for the Blind of India, recently:

"Blindcraft has been a pioneering work of great value, and we, the humble workers for the blind in a far-away land, cannot express adequately, our appreciation. We salute you for your marvelous achievements."

Blindcraft's major objective has been the giving of opportunity to blind persons, to work for an adequate wage. Blindcrafters do no begging. All their wares are sold in cooperation with merchants.

Here are a few of Blindcraft's accomplishments:

—First organization in San Francisco to offer the blind, *and otherwise handicapped,* persons, gainful employment as an alternative to begging.

—Sponsorship of San Francisco's White Cane Ordinance, and the acceptance of the white cane by blind persons as a safety measure.

—First organization to set up a memorial fund to provide last rites, when needed, by blind persons.

—First organization to care for the pre-school blind baby.

—Employment of field secretaries, who visit recently-blinded persons and help smooth the road of adjustment to life without sight.

—Extension of financial aid to blind persons who cannot work.

—Education of the public to buy Blindcraft products because of their value—not out of sympathy.

—Proving to a skeptical world that blind, and otherwise handicapped persons, could compete successfully with sighted labor in the manufacture of useful articles of highest quality which could be sold with an *unconditional money-back guarantee.*

Says Mrs. John D. Daly, first vice-president of *The San Francisco Association for the Blind,* who for years was one of Ruth Quinan's most whole-hearted supporters:

"Without prayer, the obstacles that faced the growing Blindcraft organization would have been insurmountable. Prayer not only made everything work out right, but turned many vexations into inspirations. Thousands of blind persons all over the world thank God daily that Ruth Quinan, through Blindcraft, brought the light of hope, and the warmth of faith, into their 'houses of the night.' "

Says Bob Miller, Ruth Quinan's successor as business manager: "We carry on as 'the boss' taught us—in prayer, and faith, and love."

A LBINA SHIPYARD, of Portland, Oregon," said the late Secretary of the Navy, Frank Knox, in 1943, "is unique. Here is a privately-owned yard that accepts no government subsidies, pays taxes on every dollar earned, has the lowest absenteeism rate in wartime industry, has broken every subchaser-building record, and turns out fast, sleek craft equipped with marvelously acute detection devices and mechanical ears that trace the underwater boat's course no matter how devious."

After mentioning many Albina innovations that helped reduce absenteeism from 11 per cent to 2.95 per cent, Knox said:

"When workers complained about high fruit and vegetable prices, Albina persuaded farmers to bring their produce right up to yard gates at shift-change times. Typical result: Albina employees bought peaches at $2.00 a box, which sold elsewhere for $2.89."

"Prayer Always Works," the story of Albina's Farmers' Market, was written by Mildred Lake at the request of the late Frank Knox, and is part of the Navy's records.

Prayer Always Works

I ACCEPT ANSWERS to prayer as naturally as I accept God's sunshine and showers. What I marvel at, however, is the manner in which some prayers are answered. God seems to supply a stimulus—some little incident that leads to another, and another, until a city-wide, state-wide or nation-wide movement is under way.

An answer of that kind came to me in Portland, Oregon, in 1943. I was social and financial adviser to employees of Albina Shipyard, and I came to know problems of workers and their families as few could know them. One of the things that troubled me was how to help workers with families meet their expenses.

During the first year of the war, it was possible for a shipyard worker with a large family to live on his weekly pay check. But by spring of 1943, rising prices had caught up with income, and if a man had three or more children, he could not maintain them properly in Portland on the standard wage of $62.40 a week.

Manpower was short and every worker was needed, but families who found the pay check inadequate began drifting back to their homes in other parts of the country—homes from which they'd been lured by the mirage of high wartime earnings. Albina officials tried every persuasion to keep these men on the job. Overtime work was scheduled when possible, but Albina, the only shipyard in the United States that accepted no government subsidies, operated so efficiently that little overtime was necessary.

Frequently when a good workman gave notice, the superintendent would telephone me and say: "I'm sending a man to see you. Says he can't get by on his wages. Wants to quit and go back home. He's a good man, and we don't want to lose him. Can you help him?"

I'd have the man bring his wife with him to my office, and we'd go over their expenditures. At first, by adjusting the household budget we could usually make savings. But as time went on and prices of uncontrolled commodities soared, budget adjustments became more and more futile.

One morning a welder named Price Willcoxen, came with his wife to see me. "Mrs. Lake," he said, "I make $62.40 a week. We live in a defense housing project. I ride to work on a bus. We have four children, and we're expecting a new one. We've cut our expenses to the bone, but we can't make the pay check cover our needs. I feel I've got to quit Albina, and get back home before we get so far in the hole that we'll never get out."

Mrs. Willcoxen handed me her weekly budget. These were her figures:

Victory tax, $3.15; War bond deduction, $6.25; income tax, $6.30; rent, $10.48; food, $24.00; clothing and medical care, $7.00; donations to Red Cross, War Chest, etc., 50c; Price's bus fare, $1.25; fare for Bob, to and from school, 50c; union dues, 90c; old age and accident deductions, 18c; hospitalization deduction, 50c. Total: $61.01.

"That leaves us," Mrs. Willcoxen said, "$1.29 for haircuts, light and gas bills, replacing broken dishes, odds and ends—and a movie once-in-a-while."

I studied her budget carefully. There seemed only two items on which they might economize: the food bill, and bond deductions.

"We're buying the bonds," she explained, "so we can cash them to pay the cost of having the new baby. I buy the cheapest cuts of meat, and lowest grades of canned foods. I don't know how we can cut the food bill a single penny. We live mostly on vegetables—and the cost of vegetables and fruits has gone so high that we just can't carry on."

"I know," I said.

"This morning," Mrs. Willcoxen said, "I paid forty cents for a cauliflower. I paid fifteen cents for just one peach. A small head of cabbage costs twenty-five cents—sometimes more. The doctor says we all need lots of fresh vegetables. Even nasty, wrinkled little carrots—two cents each." A tear rolled down her cheek.

My husband was director of employee and public relations at Albina. He was also public relations director of the War Materials Office of the Navy's Shipbuilding Division. He worked sixteen hours a day.

Al's and my offices were in the same building, and I went into his office to ask him to come back with me to talk to the Willcoxens.

"It wouldn't do any good, Mildred," he said. "There's nothing I can do about high food prices. Take it up with the OPA, or somebody."

"*I* think you *could* do something, Al," I said. "If fruit and vegetable prices could be held down to fair levels, these families could save four dollars on food each week—twenty dollars a month. That twenty dollars would mean the difference between going into the hole, and breaking even. These men with families don't expect to be able to save money, but they're surely entitled to the right to be able to live on their wages."

Impatiently, Al said, "Well, lots of people seem to."

"It's the fruit and vegetable prices I wish you'd do something about, Al," I said. "They're outrageous."

"Take it easy, Honey," he said. "I'm up to my neck in a *real* problem." He picked up a sheaf of reports, and sat absorbed. He looked weary. I thought: Maybe it isn't right that I try to pile more work on him. But he could *do* something about high prices if he would.

I breathed a small, silent prayer, and felt at once that everything would work out. Al—or someone else capable of solving the problem—would get interested.

I went back to my office and assured the Willcoxens that something would be done very soon about prices of fruits and vegetables. They were heartened and grateful.

Next afternoon as Al and I were about to leave for home, a worker brought me a basket of big, fresh-boiled shrimps. As Al let me out of our car at the entrance to the apartment house where we lived, I said, "Honey, do you mind going across the street and buying a head of lettuce? We're going to have fresh shrimp salad in a moment."

Al seldom went into grocery stores in those days, and began to grunt a protest—then smiled, instead. I ran up the steps with the shrimps, and was chopping celery when he banged into the apartment, plumped a head of lettuce on the table and said angrily:

"Twenty-nine cents! How long's a head of lettuce like that been costing twenty-nine cents?"

"Why, Al," I said. "That's a beautiful head of lettuce."

"Twenty-nine cents!" he said. "I used to get bigger heads of lettuce than that for a dime!"

I didn't say a word. Al was angry, and when he gets angry, something usually happens.

He brooded for a while, then went to the telephone and began calling farmers. Later, while eating the shrimp salad, he said:

"Growers are getting only three to four cents for a head of lettuce. They get sixty cents for a lug of peaches. They're paid eight cents for a medium-sized cabbage; nine cents for a large cauliflower. About one cent for three carrots. What've you been paying for peaches?"

"Almost three dollars a lug," I said.

"Five hundred per cent increase between grower and retailer," Al said. "Other items have a spread of from two hundred to four hundred per cent. A businessman's entitled to a profit, but not to that much profit. I don't know who's responsible—the commission man, the wholesaler, the retailer, or all of them—and I don't care. I'm going to do something about it."

Al went back to the telephone and arranged to take over a square block of land that Albina'd been holding for an emergency parking lot. Then he called farmers again. As we drove back to work that evening, he said:

"Mildred, we're about to open the Albina Farmers' Market. Growers will bring their produce to the yard and sell direct to workers. They'll sell at legitimate retail prices." He grinned at me sheepishly. "Surprised?" he asked.

"Of course not," I said. "I prayed about this."

"You did? When?"

"When you were too busy yesterday, to talk to Mr. and Mrs. Willcoxen. I even asured *them* that something would be done about it."

"Well, then," Al said, "the market will be successful."

At daylight next morning, farmers' trucks loaded with produce began driving into the new market. When the "graveyard" shift went off duty at 8 A.M., twenty trucks were displaying wares. Under Al's enthusiastic management, buying became hectic. Potatoes sold by the gunny sack. So did corn and squash. One grower with a flatbed loaded with peaches at two dollars a lug, sold out in less than fifteen minutes.

The day shift, streaming toward the Albina entrance gates,

saw the moderately-priced produce, and joined the buying spree. Within one hour, there was nothing left to buy.

Farmers returned with fresh supplies in the afternoon to catch the day shift coming off. Arriving swing-shifters lugged bargains to their cars in parking lots.

Albina workers spread the news, and next morning even housewives from other sections of the city were on hand when the trucks arrived. Again, farmers sold out within the hour. Twenty-four hours after the first sale at the new market, fruit and vegetable prices in the Portland area had dropped forty per cent.

The market grew beyond expectations. In time it was selling rebuilt alarm clocks and washing machines, Easter lilies, Christmas trees and other items that workers often found it difficult to buy. Albina Market made arrangements with shoemakers to give Albina workers three-day service, as compared to two-week service in most shoe repair shops. Many other innovations were introduced to help workers stay on their jobs.

Opposition to the market on the part of downtown merchants had ended before the first month had passed, and many merchants became boosters. The story of the market was given national coverage by newspapers. *Time* magazine mentioned it. As a result, similar markets were started in many war-work areas. Wherever such markets were established, absenteeism dropped, and morale improved noticeably.

When its need was over, Albina Market closed. Food prices in Portland never again got so far out of line during the war.

The success of Albina's Farmers' Market was only one of many testimonials to the efficacy of prayer at Albina. Problems of finance, morale, and labor-management relations arose every day. It is well known, throughout the shipbuilding world, that all such problems were settled quickly and satisfactorily through prayer.

L. R. Hussa, Albina's president, was a praying man. So were most department heads. Such leaders attracted many of the same type of workers, and that, I believe, is why Albina received four Navy Efficiency "E" awards for its work—the only shipyard in the United States to be so honored.

D R. *MAX RADIN, one-time professor of law at the University of California, has said that the attitude of a big section of the American people toward law is one of fear and ignorance, masked by derision.*

That attitude, surveys show, is slowly changing. It is changing because, today 96 per cent of judges in our higher courts are men who pray. This has not always been so.

Just as Judge Goodwin Knight's prayers prevented scandalous testimony in the infamous Hollywood divorce case mentioned in "The Right Answer," so the prayers of judges everywhere, are more and more directing court judgments and decisions.

When Judge Harold Medina was driven almost to a breakdown by tactics of lawyers and defendants in the trial of Communist Party leaders, he found encouragement and strength in prayer.

Tom C. Clark, associate justice of the Supreme Court of the United States, when asked about prayer, said:

"Prayer is a source of character and strength. Prayer is power."

I could quote hundreds of praying judges, but I'll let Presiding Judge Theresa Meikle, of San Francisco Superior Court—the only woman in California history to have been chosen for such a position— speak for all of them.

As I sat in Judge Meikle's office discussing prayer one day recently, she pointed to the door that lead from her chambers to her courtroom, and said:

"I never pass through that door to hold court without asking God to imbue me with sympathy, insight, and sound judgment. In court, I maintain an attitude of prayer, and let God direct my decisions."

The Right Answer

NOT SO MANY years ago, Everett Jansen, a restaurant owner in Los Angeles, built a hole-in-the-wall "beanery" into a large and profitable business because he took Jesus Christ into partnership—literally. Previously, with apparently ample capital, he'd tried to conduct a large restaurant without Jesus Christ's aid, and had failed.

In the successful partnership, Jesus was the adviser. Jansen followed His instructions, and did the workaday jobs. Each morning before he went to market at 3 A.M. to do his buying, he shut his eyes briefly and asked: "Jesus, what would You have me do today?"

Then he'd begin the day's activities, seemingly without a care. When faced with a dilemma, Jansen would pause and silently ask Jesus' advice. Answers came in many ways. Sometimes they came through overheard conversations; sometimes they came as a feeling of compulsion. But generally, the answer was ready at hand. Jansen merely asked himself: "What would Jesus do?"

Many of Jansen's customers ate at his restaurant because as soon as they stepped through the entrance they felt—as one man described it—a surge of tranquility. On the surface, the dining room was like that of the average restaurant. Dishes clattered, silverware jangled, voices rose and fell. There were sudden bursts of laughter. People jostled one another. Yet beneath the briskness and activity, was spiritual quiet.

When California's governor, Goodwin Knight, first met Jansen, he was a Los Angeles Superior Court Judge. He'd been under unusual strain because of a protracted divorce suit involving a nationally-known Hollywood couple. Attorneys for the husband had been insisting on introducing scandalous testimony that, if made public, would have besmirched the lives of the couple's two small children. Knight had refused to let the testimony be introduced in open court. Pressure was brought to bear to make Knight change his stand—heavy pressure.

One day as Knight sat in Jansen's restaurant, toying with the food, Jansen came over to him and said: "You look worried, Judge, so you must be faced with a problem."

Knight nodded.

"There can be but one right answer to any problem, Judge," Jansen said, "so there's no sense in worrying."

"True," Knight said, "there's but one right answer; the problem is to find that right answer."

"Forgive me, Judge," Jansen said, "but I must contradict you. Finding the right answer is no problem at all. Just ask yourself: 'What would Jesus do?'" Jansen smiled, then walked away.

Knight sat staring after him, then, a bit defiantly, asked himself: "Well, what *would* Jesus do?"

The answer came instantly. The strain fell from Knight. He ate hurriedly, impatient to get back to the courtroom so they could work out the solution in Jesus' way.

Knight called the principals and their attorneys into his chambers and suggested that all forget themselves; forget the bitterness and the maliciousness. "Let's drop every thought but one for exactly sixty seconds," he said. "During those sixty seconds, let's think only of the children."

He took out his watch. The principals in the case dropped

their eyes. At the end of the minute, Knight said, "Well?"
No one spoke—for words were not needed.

A settlement was agreed upon; Knight granted the divorce,
and the scandalous evidence was not mentioned again.

Since that day, on the Bench, in business, and in politics,
Knight has never made a decision without first asking—as
Saul asked on his journey to Damascus—"What shall I do,
Lord?"

Knight says with earnestness that if any man will ask that
question from his heart, he will receive his answer. "In this
impatient world," he says, "there may be times when the
answer seems long in coming, but if one keeps in tune with
the divinity within one's self, the answer will come eventually and unmistakably."

To get back to Everett Jansen, here is his story as he later
told it to Knight:

"Judge," he said, "my first big restaurant failed because
I didn't understand how to pray. Instead of asking Jesus
what to do, I'd plead with Him to help me do something
that *I* wanted to do. I used to pray that He'd help me save
my pride, humble my enemies, outsmart my competitors. I
used to spend long, weary hours after I'd gone to bed at
night, working out some scheme or other, then I'd kneel and
ask Jesus to help me put it over.

"I slept poorly, ate poorly. I became nervous and irritable.
I felt that none of my prayers was really answered. I became
bitter and despondent. I fought with my suppliers. My help
became so jittery that customers felt it, and stayed away. My
efforts and prayers became more frantic. The day came at
last, when customers were so few that I had to close the
doors.

"I opened a little beanery down on Main Street. Business
was slow, and I had time to think. I realized, gradually, that
my prayers had become only routine supplications. They'd

failed to break through the fear and misery surrounding me, and had kept my spirit from reaching through into the divine essence that fills all space.

"One evening as I sat behind an empty counter watching people—many of whom must have been hungry—walk past my little place without a glance, I suddenly felt I could endure it no longer. I realized I'd lost faith in myself, and in God. I dropped my head on my arms and cried, 'O God!'

"My cry must have been a prayer. At any rate, I grew calm, and sat there analyzing my situation. I was broke. My dream of a successful business was gone. My pride was crushed. I felt I'd lost the respect of my wife, and confidence of my friends. If ever a man was whipped, I was that man. I couldn't see how a man with my years of experience as cook, waiter, and buyer for a restaurant chain; my detailed knowledge of the intricacies of the restaurant business; my reasonable amount of capital—*could* fail—even against the hard competition among Los Angeles restaurants. Somewhere, I'd gone wrong—but where?

"It was days before I found the answer, but find it, I did. My stumbling-block was the same one that I believe thousands of Christian business men trip over every year: *I hadn't been able to reconcile Jesus' teaching of brotherly love with the bitter competition of the business world.*

"Instead of loving my competitors, I'd been hating them, tricking them, trying to force them out of business. I'd spent hours, days and months fighting, when I should have been building.

"I came to realize that the apparent successes of godless business men were only temporary, at best. I knew from my own experience that they were victims of worries, frustrations and fears. And I knew with certainty, that godless businesses must fall, finally, just as godless nations and godless leaders must fall.

"It was at this time that I found myself pausing before making even small decisions, and asking myself what Jesus would do. This resulted in improved foods for my customers —no more questionable cuts of meat, no more doubtful vegetables. I began to pretend that Jesus might drop in for lunch, and I prepared the very best food I could.

"It wasn't long before even the bums along Main Street began coming in for a bowl of really good, rich soup. Almost overnight, my little beanery became too small for the increased trade. And because I was now proud of the foods I served, my attitude toward my customers became that of a true host.

"Then a day came when because of higher cost of better foods, I had to raise prices. I thought this might be hazardous, for most of my customers were folk with little money. I prayed about it. The answer came so quickly that at first, I didn't recognize it. A seedy-looking, depressed individual ordered a bowl of Scotch broth. The broth contained the juices of many soup bones, and was heavy with barley. And it was piping hot. The man pushed back his empty bowl with a sigh, and said to me:

" 'Brother, that put new life into me. It'd be cheap at twice the price.'

"Well, the rest of my story tells itself. With Jesus' advice, I've built the business as you know it, Judge. I taught my help to let Jesus make decisions for them, too. The business is a happy one; my help is happy; our customers seem happy when they're with us. Every day, of course, brings its quota of problems—some rather difficult, too. But we're never disturbed; we're assured that our Adviser will help us solve them."

Everett Jansen believed that all minds are God's, and that when one keeps in tune with Divine Power, through prayer —spoken or unspoken—the Power directs all conscious and unconscious activities, shaping and energizing events so that no failure is possible.

Jansen said once to Knight, "With Jesus directing one's business, there's no fear, no uncertainty, no darkness. Jesus said: 'I am the light of the world: he that followeth me shall not walk in the darkness, but shall have the light of life.' When we operate in accordance with God's laws, a divine warmth and brightness permeates us; we are filled with peace. And financial rewards from businesses conducted as Jesus directs, are definite and certain, for in His own words, 'the laborer is worthy of his hire.' "

THERE IS nothing that true hot-rodders resent more than to hear harum-scarum traffic violators and speeders referred to as "hot-rodders." Genuine hot-rodders not only observe all safety regulations, but, from time to time, suggest new ones. The attitude of real hot-rodders toward the spurious ones is summed up in the following resolution adopted by officials of the Campbell Boys' Club:

We believe that highway speeders and traffic violators are suffering from mental disturbances, and that when they are apprehended for such violations, they should be restrained from driving cars until they have been treated and pronounced cured . . .

This resolution never found its way into public print, although it was submitted to newspapers. However, the belief stated in the resolution has since been acknowledged as true by many leading psychologists.

Treatment in the cases of such mentally-disturbed youths, say authorities, is well begun when the offender joins a properly supervised hot-rod club.

Hot Rods, Warm Hearts — and Prayer

THIS IS A STORY of cause and effect. Some mothers prayed; God changed the hearts of sixty teen-age "bad" boys, and ended a condition of small-town hoodlumism that had persisted for more than eight years despite all efforts of parents, teachers, and law-enforcement groups to stop it. Not only did God put an end to the unlawful activities of the so-called hoodlums, but He turned their group into one of the most constructive and law-abiding groups in the country.

I was one of the chief movers in the reformation of the boys, and at first, I operated against my will. Busy with article assignments requiring complete concentration to meet magazine deadlines, I wanted no part in any problem— juvenile or otherwise. I lived on the edge of town, secluded among trees, and was so single-minded in my desire to write that in more than two years I'd become acquainted with less than twenty persons in the small town. Yet I became the chief mover in the reformation of the boys' gang—a project so successful that the California State Police call it a miracle. There is no question in my mind—nor in the minds of my associates—that the inspiration and stimulus for our work came directly from God. Here's how it started:

One day in November I stood at the intersection of two main highways in Campbell, California. It was noon, and hundreds of students were coming from the large Union High School across the street. Down the block, scores of first-graders and second-graders were emerging from the grammar school.

Suddenly several teen-age hot-rodders, the mufflers on their cars wide open, careened down the street. With shrieking brakes, souped-up jalopies pulled up at the corner, and their drivers yelled greetings to giggling high-school girls. In only a few minutes, more than twenty hot-rods were parked in bunches on the streets, blocking traffic. Five motorcycles, their straight-pipe exhausts roaring, jockeyed to stops among the student groups.

A special traffic policeman at the center of the intersection looked on helplessly. The hot-rodders paid no attention to him.

The small business section opposite the schools quickly became a bedlam. Hundreds of students stood about munching lunches and drinking pop. One group began throwing empty bottles into the air. The bottles fell to the pavement, breaking into sharp-edged fragments.

Every minute or so, one of the hot-rodders took off in a screeching start and went tearing around the block; students scattered before him like frightened chickens. I realized I was watching the daily congregation of the gang that for years had made Campbell notorious as one of the worst "hoodlum-ridden" areas in the state.

I walked a block down the street and paused to watch four or five first-graders step out onto the crosswalk. They dashed back to safety as four motorcycles, two abreast, blasted past. Angry at such wanton disregard for lives, I turned the corner and was almost brushed off the curb as a dark-green hot-rod, tires screaming, swept by on the wrong side of the road.

After the lunch hour, when school had resumed and the hot-rodders were gone, I went from store to store, discussing the noontime situation with proprietors. This is what I learned:

The Campbell gang consisted of about sixty boys who'd either quit high school, or had been expelled. All were hot-rod enthusiasts. They staged their hazardous revel daily at the school corners; and late at night the area was filled with the shrieks of tires as the boys "laid the rubber" in races along the highways and on wide streets of new subdivisions.

Three or four times each week, the clanging of ambulances, or wailing of police car sirens, reminded residents that the Campbell gang was making a night of it.

Businessmen were distressed with the situation, and seemed to have lost hope that it could be improved. Some businesses had moved to other areas rather than submit to the noon-time debacle.

I talked to the high school principal. He seemed to feel that the hot-rodders were unamenable to discipline. He said the school had done all it could to straighten the boys out, but without success.

Still under unusual compulsion, I requested a meeting of the executive board of the Parent-Teacher Association. The group discussed hot-rodders with resigned hopelessness. They seemed to think that law-enforcement groups were not seriously trying to suppress the more lawless among the juveniles. I thought otherwise. At my own request, I was appointed a committee of one to work out a solution.

Annoyed at myself for putting myself in such a position, and feeling inadequate, on the way home, I prayed: "God, You take over. I'll try to let You direct things."

Later, I telephoned an interview to the county editor of the San Jose *Mercury,* in which I spoke of the hot-rod gang in unflattering terms.

Next morning, my telephone rang, and a teen-age voice asked:

"Are you the guy who said those things about us in the paper?"

"Yes," I replied.

"Well, we're not going to stand for it, see? We're not hoodlums. We're no different than other kids being pushed around by everybody."

"Come on out to my house," I said, "and let's have a talk."

"Yeah," the voice said, "we might do just that."

A few minutes later, a big black sedan entered my driveway, and four boys got out. They followed me into the house and sat staring at me, hostile and suspicious.

"I like guts," I said. "I like the way you rallied to defend yourselves. What's your side of the story?"

"What's the use?" replied one. "You older guys don't understand, and you can't do anything to help, anyway."

"Look," I said. "If you want your side explained to the world, I promise the San Jose *Mercury* will publish it. That paper wants to get to the bottom of your problems, and will do all it can to help you in any reasonable way."

The boys smiled skeptically.

So, while they listened, I called County Editor Thelma Miller. She said: "We'll run the boys' story gladly. Bring them in for an interview."

The gist of that interview was this: The boys insisted they were not hoodlums; that if there was a problem in Campbell, they themselves could clean it up. They and some fifty other boys of their age group had quit school prematurely, and found time hanging heavy in the small town. Because there was no place they could go for clean fun, they enjoyed congregating on the streets, talking and laughing and "cutting up" with others of the same age. They needed an outlet for their energies.

The boys were interested in motors. They wanted a speedway for motorcycles and hot-rods. A group of them had done pick-and-shovel work on a portion of the dry bed of Los Gatos Creek, leveled it, oiled it, and made it into a speedway. That got them off the streets; they thought the towns-people would be pleased. But the speedway was on private property, belonging to a gravel works, and the boys were asked to vacate. They were back on the streets again.

At this point in the interview, I told the boys that I was prepared to begin immediate action toward forming a youth recreation center. The fellows were enthusiastic. And, I'd revised my opinion of them and their friends. I knew by that time that they were fine young people, and I was determined to see that they got the chance they needed.

The next evening, the boys met and organized the Campbell Area Boys' Club for the purpose of promoting off-the-highway hot-rod activities. They appointed committees to solicit jobs for members, to work out a traffic safety program, to look into the matter of conducting a self-service garage, and to select adult advisers. I acted merely as an observer. All ideas originated with the boys. The meeting ran smoothly under the leadership of the newly-elected president, sixteen-year-old Bob Pierce. The group voted not to accept financial aid from any source until after the club had proved itself a worthwhile project. And following that meeting, hot-rod racing on Campbell streets stopped. The only speeders in the Campbell area, these days, are adults.

When newspapers appeared with the story of the formation of the club, things really began to happen. First, mothers telephoned me. Each said about the same thing:

"I've prayed for something like this. Today I'm thanking God. My boy came home last night feeling that there's a place for him in today's world, after all. God bless you—and all the others who are helping."

A retired San Jose merchant, who for forty years has been helping troubled boys, said, "I offer my full time to the boys in any way I can be of service." The boys put him to work as financial adviser.

Ezra M. Ehrhardt, officer in charge of the Safety Education Section of California Highway Patrol, said: "I offer the advice and assistance of this department—particularly in the promotion of off-the-highway activities."

The club invited Ehrhardt to speak. He did. He explained how programs had been set up in eight California cities. First, an organization of boys is formed as a nucleus, then an older group, selected by the boys, acts as adviser. Hot-rod events are staged which stress economy of performance, and reliability of vehicles. Speed is not neglected, but speed runs are made only under strict rules, and after careful checking of cars. In some hot-rod "rodeos," he said, boys have done more than a hundred miles an hour. There have been no serious accidents.

Vincent Diehl, official of the American Rifle Association, offered the boys free shooting instruction, and use of a nearby accredited rifle range.

The head of Brewer & Sons, auto body and paint shop in Cupertino, a small town near Campbell, offered to let members of the club repair their cars in his shop.

The sheriff, probation officers, and juvenile court officials personally offered encouragement and help to the club. The boys' attitude toward law enforcement immediately changed from antagonism to cooperation. The hearts of boys are easily reached.

The Reverend Corwin Olds, state chaplain of the California National Guard, and pastor of a Campbell church, arranged for the club to meet in the church social hall until the boys obtained club rooms of their own.

The boys—sixty-eight of them now—voted to turn down the offer of the Campbell High School to conduct evening classes in general shop and auto repair. They appreciated the spirit in which the school made the offer, but said that the course was too elementary for hot-rod enthusiasts—many of whom are capable of tearing down worn-out stock car engines and building into them almost twice their original efficiency. Instead, they voted to establish their own auto mechanics' school as soon as possible.

The county recreation department watched progress of the Campbell organization for about ten days, then sent an unofficial representative, interested in the possibility of creating a county-wide program, using the Campbell club as a nucleus.

Young Bob Pierce, president of the club, pointed out at a meeting to which parents and other adults were invited that the problem of hot-rodders is a national problem. He said:

"There are at least forty thousand hot-rods on the roads of California—maybe a half million of them throughout the country. But only a few hot-rod drivers are interested in speed for speed's sake. Our main interest is the improvement of car engines. Some of us can take a hack saw, a screwdriver, a file, and a wrench, and add forty horsepower to a standard Ford engine.

"But where are we to test our ideas? We've only the highways. Hot-rod traffic problems are really the result of resentment against grownups who don't understand that we need help in getting locations for our activities. Most of us are regular guys when we're given an opportunity to do things right."

Commented Officer Ehrhardt (who got the idea for his statewide safety program through prayer, and who never makes a move without asking God to direct him):

"Bob's right. It's a national problem. I believe that within five years, all states will provide facilities for expanding this program. This means places where sanctioned hot-rod and motorcycle meets can be held in safety."

Soon after the story of the formation of the Campbell Area Boys' Club hit the news wires, letters began coming from authorities in Virginia, North Carolina, and Texas, praising the boys, and requesting detailed information about the club.

So it goes. Everything working toward the common good, because of prayer.

SAYS SOIL Scientist J. E. Dunn, of "Fruitful Valley".

"If the farmers of America would prayerfully follow a soil-management program in keeping with God's plan for growing things, they would save most of the five billion dollars a year that plant diseases and insects are now costing them.

"The first step in God's plan for farming is to realize that soil is a living thing. It breathes, has a skeleton, has digestive and eliminative systems. If intelligently cared for, it becomes more productive year after year. Like a human body, soil, if mistreated too long, deteriorates, and becomes a haven for pests and diseases of all kinds. But, unlike the human body, soil does not die. No matter how starved, how neglected, it can be rebuilt by intelligent management.

"Even the poorest, most depleted soils can be restored to productivity in from two to five years, as Louis Bromfield has proved at his internationally-famed Malabar Farms near Mansfield, Ohio; and as thousands of other farmers have proved.

"Strangely, many of the fungi that destroy crops in soil-depleted fields are beneficial to those same crops when the soils are in proper balance.

"When crops are grown God's way, most of the hordes of destructive insects, fungi and bacteria now wreaking havoc on American farms would not appear at all, for they thrive only where soils are, themselves, sick from improper management."

173

Fruitful Valley

WHEN JIM DUNN first saw the Yakima Valley in Washington thirty years ago, it made his heart glad. It was harvesttime, and the trees on tens of thousands of acres were heavy with apples, peaches, pears, cherries and plums. Yakima Valley fruit was as firm, colorful, juice-filled and nutritious as any fruit in the world. From the valley's packing sheds long trains of refrigerator cars carried the fruit to the markets of the world.

Dunn made up his mind that some day he'd return to this fruitful valley and make it his home. It was an ideal spot for a soil specialist—and Dunn was one of the best.

It was fifteen years before Dunn was able to return, and what he saw then, made his heart sick. Thousands of once-proud trees were dying of rots, molds, mildews and other deficiency diseases. Yakima Valley fruit was no longer wanted in the nation's markets. In fact, the fruit had become so inferior that little of it could be shipped at all. Plums grew so small that they were little more than skin-covered pits. Apples and peaches softened a few hours after picking. Cherry trees grew emaciated caricatures of cherries. Pears suffered from hardend, premature softening, and other ills.

But let Jim Dunn tell the story in his own words:

"After seeing what man's ignorance had done to this once-fertile valley, I wanted to run away. But I'd come back to stay—and stay, I did. However, I prayed before I made my decision. I knelt to ask God to guide me in my work here. I arose from my knees knowing I had a mission to accomplish; that henceforth my knowledge, my strength, and all my resources would be devoted to helping reclaim and rejuvenate these humus-robbed, starving and disease-ridden soils. I knew I'd never leave the Yakima Valley until once again I saw it blossoming in health, producing top-grade fruit.

"It was not a one-man job. I'd have to have help. I'd have to learn to know men of faith, men of prayer. Together we could, with God's help, change the farming practices of thousands; change the thinking of a people. But where to find such men?

"Again I prayed. God directed me to a vegetable farmer named Ed Flannigan, a former big-league baseball player. Through Flannigan, I met two prominent Yakima businessmen, Harry McMurray, and Arch Deaver. Like most others in the valley, these men were greatly concerned with the tragedy of the fruit. They knew something was wrong— terribly wrong—with the farming practices of the area. But what?

"They'd asked advice from fifteen or sixteen Federal, State and County agricultural agencies, and had received fifteen or sixteen different answers. No two agencies agreed either on the cause of the trouble, or its cure.

"One ray of hope came from officials of the Federal agricultural setup in Washington, D.C. These men said: 'Rebuild your soils as they were when you first began growing fruit trees, and maintain them at that level. This means the discing-in of heavy cover crops annually.'

"However, this advice was exactly contrary to that of local agricultural officials and commercial-fertilizer distributors, who insisted that growers keep the floors of their orchards as free of vegetation as billiard tables. They assured the farmers that soil deficiencies thus created could be overcome by heavy applications of chemicals. Farmers, deeply in debt, and bewildered by contradictory advice, refused to attempt any program that involved spending a large amount of money.

"I spent months analyzing the soils of the area, and questioning growers about their specific problems. As I watched the wholesale bulldozing-out of diseased trees, my heart grew heavier and heavier. I knew that if I could persuade the orchardists to follow a program that did not violate the laws of nature, most of the trees could be saved.

"When I suggested to the orchardists that they permit me to lay out a growing program for them, they rebuffed me. Who was I? What was I selling? What right had I to give advice contrary to that of their local agricultural authorities? Those were some of the questions asked me.

"I replied that I was a soil scientist who'd opened a soil research laboratory in Yakima; that I was making a survey of the soils conditions of the area; that I would analyze their soils, and outline a soil-improvement program for which they could pay me, or not, as they chose. I explained that I had nothing to sell but my services, in helping them increase production. I even offered, in some cases, to work on a basis of 'no crop increase, no pay.' Anything, just to get things started.

"Most of the farmers laughed at me. Some of them thought I was a bit soft in the head.

"Flannigan, McMurray, Deaver and I discussed the problem at length. We decided that a campaign of education must be started; that it would probably be a long one; and that an actual orchard demonstration must be undertaken.

"We drew up a 'Save the Orchards' program, the very warp and woof of which was prayer. Flannigan dedicated his farm as a demonstration project. He followed instructions to the letter. Growers were asked to watch progress. They were told:

"*'And the earth brought forth grass, herbs yielding seed after their kind, and trees bearing fruit, wherein is the seed thereof, after their kind: and God saw that it was good.'*

"The fruit was good because it was grown in soils that God had made—soils rich in humus, alive with bacteria and other living organisms whose duty is to break down the humus into a form that can be assimilated by plants, as nutrients.

"When orchards were first planted in the Yakima Valley, the soil was very good, because they were grown in soils prepared for them by nature. Nature's way is God's way. But farmers of the Yakima Valley stopped permitting nature's food to be restored to the soil. They killed all grass and weeds and vegetative growth in their orchards. They attempted to feed the trees with artificial fertilizers—not knowing that even these can do no good unless they're broken down by chemical reactions—possible only in humus-heavy soils.

"Opposition to my program became intense. One excited agricultural official wrote to Ben Perham, a regent of State College of Washington, and one of the valley's large fruit-growers, saying that I was a fraud, and should be arrested. Perham showed me this letter, and said:

" 'I believe, Dunn, that you may be the answer to my prayers. My orchards have deteriorated until it's useless to continue with our present farming practices. Tell me briefly what you suggest for this valley.'

" 'I propose,' I said, 'to persuade growers to replace, by manuring and cover cropping, the humus of which the soils have been robbed. All your soils are deficient in lime. I want lime added at the rate of not less than two thousand pounds per acre. But every farm is an individual problem, and must have its own particular program.'

"Perham thought that over for a few minutes. Suddenly he smiled. 'Look,' he said, 'we'll confound your opposition in a practical way. I'll give you a two-acre strip down the center of my sick Winesap apple orchard. You give me a program. I'll follow it. We'll see what we'll see.'

"Two years later, I stood with Perham on his porch, and looked out at his orchard. Trees on the two-acre test-strip were dark-green, disease-free, and heavy with fruit. The trees in the rest of the orchard were sicker than ever.

"The next year, all of Perham's orchards were under soil-improvement programs.

"Meanwhile, Flannigan's farm was thriving as it had never thrived before. His products were uniform in quality and size. They graded chiefly A-1. None broke down in shipment.

"A group of men whose lives were dedicated to Christian principles met each week to talk over topics important to the area. I became a member of this group, and at informal round-table discussions we went deeply into the soil problems of the valley. These men prayed for guidance, and each became a missionary for the new deal for local fruit. Their efforts began to show results.

"First one grower, then another, and another, joined the soil-improvement program. I bought an eight-acre ranch on the edge of Yakima. It was one of the most run-down orchards in that section. The ground was almost as hard as brick. Irrigation water penetrated very slowly. The soil was so lacking in bacteria and other necessary organisms that although the former owner had used twenty times as much artificial fertilizer as ordinarily required, it didn't do a particle of good.

"We cover-cropped, disced, limed, fertilized, and cover-cropped again. The light tight, clay-like soil became darker and more friable every year. Water penetration improved, until less than one-third the water formerly used was necessary for production.

"Within five years, the fruit on this place was the delight of all who handled it. Firm, vitamin-packed, disease-free, beautifully colored, it was shipped to the farthest points without deterioration. And so it is to this day.

"The tide of public approval flowed steadily in my favor. Ten years of effort, of patience and of faith that we were cooperating in a program approved by God, paid off a thousandfold. The leader of the opposition became converted, and today he writes articles for fruit magazines, advocating the very orchard practices he once fought so bitterly.

"The growers of all that vast area are again prosperous and happy. Their trees are comparatively free of disease. Their soils are dark and redolent with humus. Mortgages have been paid off. Schools have been built. And Yakima Valley fruit is once again famous for quality the world over.

"God sustained us, and advised us, during the long fight. Through Him, a miracle was accomplished. Land once almost worthless became fruitful. Enemies became friends. Growers can say today, as did two of the men Moses sent into the valley of Eschol: 'The . . . land is an exceeding good land.' "

NOW A MEMBER of California's Advisory Agricultural Council, Jim Dunn is today working to improve farming practices in Santa Clara Valley, California, where 55,000 acres of pears, plums, apricots, peaches and cherries are infected with oak-root fungus and where other diseases threaten the existence of the berry industry. He says:

"You just can't lose—with God on your side."

THOSE WHO teach children well are more to be honored than they who produce them; for these only gave them life, those the art of living well. —Aristotle.

We shall one day learn to supersede politics by education. What we call our root-and-branch reforms of slavery, war, gambling, intemperance, is only medicating the symptoms. We must begin higher up, namely, in education. —Emerson.

He is to be educated because he is a man, and not because he is to make shoes, nails and pins. —Channing.

Story of a Schoolteacher

ONE DAY JUST after school had let out I sat beside the desk of Miss Margaret Madden, the sixty-year-old eighth-grade teacher in the small town in California whom we spoke about earlier in "The Teacher Who Learned to Pray." She and I were checking a manuscript on some phases of education that I'd written with her help. The only sounds reaching the room were from children outside shouting to each other.

Came a knock on the door, and a man walked in. I recognized him as Otis Hardinge, one of the town's two bankers. He was comparatively young, probably in his early forties. Miss Madden said, "Hello, Otis."

He nodded without speaking, and went directly to a student desk near the back of the room, sat down and closed his eyes. Miss Madden watched him for a few moments with compassion and tenderness. Then she turned back to our manuscript.

From time to time I glanced at Hardinge. He neither moved nor spoke; just sat, with eyes closed. About twenty minutes later he came to the desk, face peaceful, eyes calm. Miss Madden asked, "Well, Otis?"

He smiled. "I've got my answer," he said, and nodded to me as he walked briskly out.

For a moment, a shaft of late sunlight turned Miss Madden's silver hair into a halo. She said:

181

"Otis comes here to pray when he's faced with a difficult problem. He's been doing that for years. He's a successful man; in addition, he's one of the state's best-known amateur photographers. He sits in the same old seat that was his years ago when he was one of my pupils."

"Don't forget that I collect prayer stories, Miss Madden," I said.

"Yes, I know," she smiled. "Well, Otis learned how to pray in that old desk. He was supposed to be a problem boy. When he passed into the eighth grade, his former teachers warned me about him; said he'd cause trouble. He did. He got in a mess for which he was to have been expelled.

"One day I asked him to stay after school. He sat sullen, refusing to talk. I prayed silently for guidance, for I knew that the real Otis was a fine boy.

"After I'd prayed, I sat without speaking for quite a while. Then I said, 'Will you tell me, Otis, why you play hooky so often?'

"He glared.

"I said: 'I know there's a reason, Otis—probably a good one. I'd like to know it. Perhaps understanding your reason will help me to help other boys.'

"Otis seemed to melt. He said, 'Miss Madden, when I see snow on the mountains, I just have to go.' He flushed in embarrassment.

" 'When I see snow on the mountains, I just have to go,' I repeated. 'Why Otis, that's poetry! Tell me about the snow.'

"His eyes shone. 'I think snow pictures are beautiful,' he said. 'I take my camera and try for shadow pictures. You know, strong blacks and whites—long, dark shadows across the snow. They make me think of . . . I . . .' He stopped abruptly.

" 'I've often wished I had a good camera,' I said. 'What kind is yours, Otis? Tell me about it.'

"With warmth, he said shyly: 'I paid two hundred and forty-seven dollars for it. It's good, really good.'

"I knew that Otis's parents were poor, and that an expensive camera seemed far beyond their means. Otis seemed to know what I was thinking, for he said:

" 'I earned it myself, Miss Madden. Worked vacations in the cannery, and did odd jobs. Built a darkroom. Have an enlarger. I've got some swell pictures. Someday I'll . . .'

"I watched the light die out of his face as he realized he'd been baring his heart. I said. 'May I come and see your darkroom—and your pictures?'

" 'Would you, Miss Madden? When? Could you come now?' he asked.

"I nodded, put on my hat, and walked with Otis to his home. Bless him—he'd built a darkroom from scraps of lumber. It was fitted with a weird collection of trays, basins and gadgets he'd picked up secondhand. It was a good darkroom, nevertheless. He did excellent work. His pictures—proudly shown—revealed a true knowledge of composition, and artistic imagination. He showed me his camera, displaying it as fondly as a parent displays a baby.

"I said, 'Otis, you're not only a poet, but an artist, too. Now I understand why you play hooky—and I can't really blame you. You're doing a wonderful job with your camera. But you must finish your education, Otis. To be a great artist, you'll need what school has to give you.'

" 'They're going to expel me, anyway,' he said.

" 'Well,' I told him, 'maybe if we pray about it . . . you pray, don't you, Otis?'

" 'My mother prays,' he said, 'but . . .'

" 'Otis,' I said, 'you really pray a great deal, but you don't realize that you do. This gift you have for photography comes from God. Your gift of words comes from God. Every time you look through that finder, wishing for your lens to capture something beautiful, you're praying. Every time you develop your films, doing your best to bring out the captured beauty, you're praying. Prayer is only the sincere appeal of a heart to a Power greater than itself—the same Power that created the beauty and goodness that you capture with your camera.' I picked up three or four prints. 'These are proof that you prayed, Otis,' I said, 'and that God heard your prayers. In these prints are God's mountains and trees, His sunshine and shadows, His sky and His clouds—all part of His universe.'

"Tears misted his eyes, and I turned away. After a time, he said:

" 'I'll pray, Miss Madden. Maybe they won't expel me.'

" 'God will hear you,' I said. 'I must go now, and thanks, Otis, for a wonderful hour.' "

As Miss Madden finished speaking, I marveled at the radiance in her face. She said:

"Boys and girls are precious. In every one of them is a dream of goodness, of beauty—a dream of achievement. Once they understand that their aspirations are urgings from God, they're cooperative with authority—wonderfully cooperative.

"A few mornings later," she continued, "when the principal sent for Otis, I saw the boy close his eyes for a moment, silently praying.

"He wasn't expelled. Instead, the principal brought him back to the room, patted him on the shoulder and sent him to his seat. Then he turned to me and said:

" 'Miss Madden, we have an honor for your class. Otis has been appointed official photographer for the school.' "

Next day I went to interview Banker Otis Hardinge. He told me:

"Miss Madden, more than any other human influence, has made this town prosperous, and a good place in which to live. My own story is only one of many. She discovered that one 'bad' boy had music hidden deep within him. He's now a well-known orchestra leader. She found another was a genius at repairing engines. Today he operates our best garage. Walk down the main street, and in almost every successful business, you'll find someone in charge who was once a pupil of Miss Madden's. Somehow, she finds the good in youngsters, and brings it out. And she teaches them to pray."

ONE HUNDRED miles south of the well at Buna, the water of which saved George Clossett's life, are the seventy wells of Wajir. How and by whom these wells were dug is one of Africa's mysteries. Somalis say that the wells were dug by giants more than four thousand years ago. Fifty to sixty feet deep, the wells were drilled through solid rock; a job far beyond the capacities of present-day natives.

The Bible tells of giants that lived near that part of Africa even before Adam. Moses, in Deuteronomy 3:11, says:

"For only Og King of Bashan remained of the remnant of giants; behold, his bedstead was a bedstead of iron . . . Nine cubits [15 feet] was the length thereof, and four cubits [7 feet] the breadth of it . . ."

Sheikh Ahamed Liban, an influential Somali chieftain, says that more than fourteen billion camels and thirty billion goats have been watered at the Wajir wells since the giants dug them.

As the lives of thirty thousand natives in the vast desert area surrounding Wajir depend on camels, and the lives of the camels depend on the seventy wells, it is easy to understand why Somalis call the waters "The Waters of Life."

The Living Water Chandlery

THERE WAS A ship's chandlery business in London near the East India Docks that for many years was known as the Living Water Chandlery.

Curious about the name, and wondering if it had religious significance, I went one day and asked for the proprietor. He was a sturdy, red-faced Englishman named George Clossett. He said:

"Aye. I chose the name from St. John 4:10."

"The story of the Samaritan woman at the well, isn't it?"

"Aye. Jesus asked her for a drink of water."

"I remember," I said, then quoted: 'If thou knewest the gift of God, and who it is that saith to thee, Give me to drink; thou wouldst have asked of him, and he would have given thee living water."

"Aye. That's it."

"An unusual name for a business."

"So it is."

"Has it to do with prayer?"

"Aye."

"I collect stories of answers to prayer for a book I may write some day," I said.

"Well," he said thoughtfully, "if you're willing to listen, I'm willing to tell. Come back into the office."

I sat down at a table used as a desk, but Clossett stood, looking down at me. He said:

"It was that I was sick in my soul. My spirit was parched for lack of God's living water, but I did not know it. What I did know was that this business, once so prosperous, had become a mockery. It was not only losing money, but the list of fine, solid customers it had acquired through two lifetimes had given place to a clientele of questionable character.   ,

"This business had been owned by my father, and by his father before him—Christian men who conducted the business as unto God. Their names were of good report among shipping men in every port in the world. They had immense pride in the wares they sold, and wanted them used only in honest ventures. When merchandise left this place, they'd place their hands on each shipment and say, 'Go with God.' "

Clossett pulled a chair toward him with his foot, sat down and look at me quizzically.

"Does that sound odd?" he asked.

"No. It's a fine prayer."

"Well," he said, "in course of time the business fell to me. For some years prior to that time, I'd been impatient with my father because of his practice of refusing to sell except to men of good repute. There was a deal of illegitimate shipping in those days: smuggling, fish-poaching, and that sort of thing. Right here along the Thames were hundreds of small craft engaged in lawless enterprises. I'd felt that by refusing to sell to such persons we were foolishly passing up big profits. I prided myself on being a 'modern' businessman, so I let word get about that I would sell to any and all.

"Within one year, business doubled. But a strange thing happened. I found that I could not lay my hands on shipments and say, 'Go with God.'

"I tried it, aye. I thought of it as a sort of rite that went with the business. But I tried it only once, for the words stuck in my throat.

"Now, a man can't be reared in an atmosphere of godliness and easily shrug it off. I reminded myself that the code of modern business was one of *laissez faire;* I must be tolerant of what people chose to do with merchandise they bought from me. But I grew increasingly unhappy. Bible passages that had once inspired me seemed flat and depressing. It was not long before I'd convinced myself that God and business would not mix.

"I continued to make sales—far more sales than my father had made. But the dignity—aye, the nobility—of the business had vanished. Gone also was peace of spirit, the sense of well-being. Firms who'd been customers for generations went elsewhere to trade."

Clossett went to an old-fashioned safe, took out a large, heavy ledger, put it unopened on the table, and rested his hand on it.

"In this ledger," he said, "are accounts running back over sixty years. Almost all accounts in those days were paid quarterly. Some totaled thousands of pounds. Yet there is not a single account of that period which remains unsettled."

From a shelf Clossett took a smaller ledger. "This," he said, "contains the accounts during my first two years." He held the book before me and leafed through the pages. There were many red-ink entries. "Unpaid accounts," he said, "many of them. During those two years I increased sales almost two hundred and fifty per cent. And I also lost more money through bad accounts than my father and grandfather lost in more than half a century.

"In ignorance, y' see, I'd believed that business is something separate from God. I'd thought the old rules of business had changed with our changing economy. But finally I realized that business is always subject to God's laws as is everything else on earth. Those laws were established in the beginning, and they're as unchangeable as is God Himself."

Clossett put the ledgers away, and went on:

"It wasn't the loss of money that drove me to near-despair at that time. It was the realization that in ignorant self-sufficiency, I was destroying a business that was good and true—a benefit to mankind. I felt that my father had left me pearls, and I'd cast them before swine.

"I was an uncertain and humiliated man as I went to each of my father's old customers, one by one, and asked for their business again. But they'd made new contacts, and did not intend to break them.

"I was not bankrupt, but driven by an urge to escape, I closed the doors of the business and obtained a commission in the army.

"And I prayed, but without faith. I read and re-read my father's favorite Bible verse, but without feeling: 'If thou knewest the gift of God, and who it is that saith to thee, Give me to drink; thou wouldst have asked of him, and he would have given thee living water.'

"The truth is that I was dying of spiritual thirst, but my soul remained parched.

"Eventually, because I possessed special knowledge, the army sent me to Biricau in Italian Somaliland to arrange for shipments of acacia gums, hayewood, and haskul fibers. It became necessary that I make a trip beyond Buna, in the Northern Frontier District of Kenya. That is more than three hundred miles through a country so hot and dry as to be almost unbelievable. We journeyed by camel train to that land of scarce water and vanishing grass—land so drenched in baking heat during the day that the wandering Somalis travel only at night. And they go no farther than fourteen days' travel from the dog-leg well at Buna, for fourteen days is about the limit of a camel's ability to go without water.

"Sixty miles northwest of Buna, our party was attacked by

bandit Somalis. We fought them off, but all but one of our camels were killed, and the precious water they'd carried on their backs in giraffeskin bags was lost. The surviving camel carried only enough water for two small mouthfuls twice a day for me and my party.

"I won't dwell on that desperate journey to Buna except to say that we lay a-thirst in the meager shade of desert scrub each day, lips cracked, tongues swollen, obsessed by visions of cool, running water. At night we shuffled forward, moaning in unison with the pitiful crying of our lone camel.

"The night before we reached Buna, in lucid intervals I heard myself praying. This was my prayer: 'Living water. Living water.'

"When about two miles out of Buna, we were seen stumbling, falling, getting up again to stagger forward. Two black soldiers of the King's African Rifles rushed to our aid and brought water. The only way I can describe my sensations as I gulped that blessed water is to say that it seemed a cool breeze began blowing softly through each muscle of my body. My mind cleared; strength surged through me. Relief was so intense that I wept.

"Ordinarily our camel would have had to wait his turn at the water-troughs while beasts that had arrived earlier, drank. But the soldiers let him drink at once, led him away; then in an hour or so, they took him back to drink his fill.

"Several days were required to gather together a new camel outfit. While my sergeant dickered with Somalis for good beasts and equipment, I, fascinated and prayerful, stood for hours near the well, watching cattle, goats and camels drinking at the troughs, watching the two Somali women who stood on the slippery slopes of the well walls, pulling up giraffe-hide buckets at the ends of ropes—buckets that, far underground, had been filled on the lower slope of the dog-leg and passed from hand to hand by ten or twelve other Somalis. And all day long, as the buckets moved from hand to hand, the passers chanted a song of praise to the waters.

"I thought of the mystery of that well. Dug through solid rock, its sides were as clean and as smooth as if bored by machinery. The well was thousands of years old. Were the men who dug it—as the Somalis believe—really giants?

"I watched herds of hump-backed cattle, dirty gray camels, and irascible goats wait their turns to be called to the troughs. I watched them drink their fill and move mournfully off and out into the desert again to hunt for grass so sparse that it barely maintained life.

"At night I'd hear the camel-bells as herds moved in from the outer darkness—goats bleating, cattle mourning, camels howling—thirst-stricken, every one.

"And that is how I came to know what Jesus had meant when He spoke of 'living water.' "

Clossett paused. "That's about all. I regained health, and found that skepticism and conceit had been burned out. And ever since, my constant prayer has been that I remain filled with the living water of God.

"When my army service ended, I reopened and renamed the business. The business has prospered. Aye, the name, Living Water Chandlery, has been more than a name; it's a prayer."

Clossett rose. We shook hands.

"Go with God," he said.

SINCE the experience related in "Experiment in Faith," I've met several men who lend money to the needy without asking references or security, and without charging interest. In every case, the losses from unrepaid loans average less than one-half of one per cent.

Most interesting of the lenders is a retired Chicago contractor, who lends small sums to young married couples.

He eliminates dishonest would-be borrowers by the simple expedient of asking them to kneel with him in his office and pray that God will bless the loan.

"Every so often," he told me, "someone gets up from his kneees and says: 'I can't pray about this. I haven't been honest with you.' I have found that few men," he said, "will pray for God's help in a crooked deal."

Most of this contractor's loans are made to Negroes—supposedly poor risks; yet except in a very few instances all borrowers have paid up. Loans are never for more than fifty dollars, and repayment installments are often as low as fifty cents a week.

"Some day," this contractor said, "bankers will realize that prayer is the best security of all.'

Experiment in Faith

ONE COLD, SLEETY, gusty afternoon in December 1942, Jake Skeen, a thirty-year-old Louisiana sharecropper, parked his battered jalopy close to the main gate of Albina Shipyard in Portland, Oregon, just as one of the back tires collapsed with a discouraged groan.

It was a little after four o'clock, and the shipyard lights were turned on in preparation for a dismal night. Skeen got out of the car and examined the flat tire. It was beyond repair, and Skeen stood hunched against the gusts with tears of frustration in his eyes.

In the front seat, his shivering wife stared dully at the wet hulls glistening on the ways. In the back seat, a boy of ten and a girl of six huddled together under a soggy quilt. Beside them, wrapped in an old gray blanket, a ten-month-old baby slept.

For the Skeens, it was the end of a long, weary trail. They were dirty, damp, hungry and ragged. They were homeless, penniless, and without ration stamps for gas. They had no hope of shelter against the night.

A gate guard brought the family into the Employees and Public Relations Office, where I told them to huddle close to the electric heater while the guard went to the shipyard restaurant for hot soup, and for warm milk for the baby's bottle.

When the guard came back, the baby took its bottle and gurgled happily. The others drank their soup from the bowls in noisy, greedy gulps. My wife Mildred, my assistant, watched them with compassion. I'd seen that look in her eyes many times during the past few weeks, for the plight of the Skeen family was the plight of many families in Portland.

Lured by newspaper ads calling for workers for a group of shipyards, men from all parts of the United States had gathered up their families, and migrated to Portland. Hundreds of them had used their savings to make the trip, only to find when they arrived that there was no housing for them, and no job unless they had money to pay union initiation fees in advance. With no jobs, there was no money to buy welding clothes, helmets, groceries; no money to pay rent for a temporary hotel room; no money to buy gas for the car.

Skeen told us that after he learned he could not work in any of the shipyards that had advertised for help, he'd applied for work at other war-industry plants. Knowing that Albina had no labor shortage, he'd come there last. He needed eighty dollars to stake him until payday.

As a shipyard, Albina was unique. It operated on its own money, and refused government financing of its war orders. Albina prospered because it was directed by men who prayed—men like President L. R. Hussa and Treasurer E. W. Erren.

The growing number of jobless migrants who showed up at Albina's gates begging for work and enough money to tide them over until they earned enough to finance themselves, rested heavily on officials' hearts.

That December evening as the Skeens crowded close to the heater's glowing coils, Mildred seemed to have reached a decision. She picked up the baby, cuddled it, and said:

"Al, there's no decent reason why all these people who come here in such straits shouldn't be given jobs and lent sufficient money to see them in the clear. They're people—they need help. Albina should give it."

"But, Mildred," I said, "we've no jobs. Albina has a waiting list of workers. We're operating at full capacity."

"Jobs will be available," she said. "I've prayed about this, Al. I know I'm right."

"But," I said, "we can't lend Albina's money to just anybody who comes along. We'd lose . . ."

"Oh, hush!" she said. "Have you so little faith?"

"Well," I said, "I don't feel like assuming the responsibility. We'd have to lend thousands of dollars to stake every destitute family that shows up here."

"Then I'll talk it over with Mr. Erren," she said. And she did.

To my astonishment, Mr. Erren came to our office next morning, put us in his car and took us to a bank where he opened a special checking account and told us to go ahead and lend money as we saw fit.

I called one of Portland's biggest bankers, for advice. He said the idea was crazy; he prophesied a loss of from forty to sixty per cent. Our auditor was as opposed to the plan as the banker. The superintendent, however, liked the idea, and promised to create jobs for as many as he could.

Opposition to the plan came from other shipyards, and from petty officials at Albina. They said the proposed loan set-up was unethical, and would lower workers' morale in the whole area. Mr. Hussa, however, who saw only the good in any situation, let the opposition dash itself against the rock of his faith in the inherent goodness of men.

And so began an experiment unique in American industry. Men who did not have the money to buy the right to work, who'd uprooted their families, and had no money to return to their old homes, or to support new ones, were financed until they could stand on their own feet.

Albina found them apartments or rooms, guaranteed their rent; guaranteed their bills for welding clothes, paid their union initiation fees, and lent them money for groceries and family necessities. No character references were required and no security was asked. The borrowers were not even required to work at Albina if they preferred working elsewhere.

The men made arrangements to repay the loans in small weekly sums—the size of the payments depending on the size of the family. Mildred handled all transactions. She did no preaching, pointed no moral. But she managed to impress on each borrower that she had perfect faith in him—or rather, that she had faith in the Christ within every man's heart.

Mildred was no starry-eyed dreamer; she was neither naïve nor gullible. She was one of America's outstanding public relations executives. She conducted her departments as she thought Jesus would have her do, and she went ahead lending Albina's money with serene confidence, despite opinions of some minor executives and influential money-changers of Portland.

So the jobless borrowed: hundreds upon hundreds of them. Most were solid citizens who tried to do the best they knew how, but some were pretty questionable characters. Among these were former gangsters, slickers, deadbeats, hoodlums and assorted rascals. Mildred lent to them all. They'd enter her office haggard with worries, and leave with faces so alight with relief and gratitude that they seemed transformed.

Bookkeeping records show that Mildred lent in excess of $166,000. Losses? *Less than one-tenth of one per cent.* When the books were closed on the loans, only two men had failed to pay. Both were institutional cases, and Albina forgave the debts.

While the experiment was a remarkable testimony to the good that dwells in every man, the repayment of the loans was a minor part of the good that came from the Albina plan. Morale among Albina workers reached a peak so high that absenteeism dropped from eleven per cent to 2.95 per cent— the lowest in the United States. Albina workers subscribed a total per man for war bonds that was nine times greater than that of the total per man in any other war plant. Albina workers broke every subchaser-building record. Albina athletic teams won every war-industries sports championship. Albina's flag carried four Navy efficiency stars—an honor accorded no other American shipyard. Because Albina had proved it could accomplish the seemingly impossible, the government appointed this firm its expediter for war materials for thirty-five other subchaser yards, and for the government's own submarine-building bases.

Albina's remarkable *ésprit de corps,* radiating from the nucleus of men who'd come there destitute and who, having asked for bread, were not given a stone, even inspired the crews of the subchasers. Said the late Secretary of the Navy, Frank Knox, to a meeting of labor leaders in Pittsburgh:

"Albina has done as much to improve the morale of the Navy as any other single influence since Pearl Harbor."

After checking the books on Albina's loan set-up, the skeptical banker said: "I admit you've lost less money on loans to workers than we, with all our caution, lost during the same period. You did a good job, but I don't like the way you drag God into it."

Mildred's eyes flashed. "God, not man," she said, "made the laws that govern successful business. When you search for rules that enable you to conduct your business so it thrives, you're really searching for God. You're seeking to know His will. Obedience to God's rules for business is the only way to *lasting* success."

*I*N NEW ORLEANS *a few years ago I interviewed a Negro named Tom Seymour because I'd heard that Seymour's prayers were always answered. He was a gray-haired old fellow, and worked in a bakery. I explained to him that I collected prayer stories, and that I'd like to write about him and prayer. He said:*

"Why, man, there ain't nothing to write about me. I just got one kind of prayer. That's all—just one kind."

"Maybe your prayer will help others," I said.

"For goodness sakes!" he said. "It's just a little, old prayer. I just look inside me and pray."

"Inside you?"

"Yes, sir. That's where God is—in my heart."

"And your prayer is always answered?"

"Yes, sir. God tells me what He thinks I ought to do. That's all I ask Him. I just say: 'God, you're right there, and You can see what I ought to do, so please tell me.' And He always does. Like right now. I just prayed that God would tell me what to say to you, because you sort of got me flustered—writing about me, and all that."

"You got an answer?"

"Yes, sir. God wants me to say that if people didn't pray so far off, everybody'd always get answered. God wants you to write that He's in everybody's heart—and that's just as close as He can get."

The Man Who Learned
to Mind His Own Business

IN THE SUMMER of 1952 I visited Adlai Stevenson's campaign plane at Portland, Oregon, to interview him for a national magazine. Among the men around Stevenson was an influential Tennessean named Marvin Rice, whom I recognized as a man I'd interviewed in 1923 aboard the *S.S. Empress of Canada* as she lay at her pier in Vancouver, British Columbia.

Rice recognized me too, although we'd both become gray with the years. We shook hands, and Rice said:

"I never saw the story you wrote about me."

"It was never published," I told him. "I was marine editor of the Vancouver *World*. Remember? When I turned your story in to the managing editor, he said, 'Lake, you're a shipping editor—not a church editor.' Your story went into his wastebasket."

Rice opened his billfold, and through the transparent window of the card compartment I read these words: *"Remember January 15, 1921."*

I said, "So you've carried that reminder all these years, Rice!"

"Yes, and they've been happy, prosperous years," Rice said.

A few weeks later I dug into old files and re-read my notes on the Vancouver interview. Here's that long-unpublished story, told for the first time:

A passenger list for the then new *S.S. Empress of Canada* was being made up, and Miss Gaw, of the Canadian Pacific Railway's publicity department, telephoned to give me names of passengers whom she thought might make interesting stories for the paper.

She mentioned several socially-prominent persons, then added, "You might find a story in a bachelor named Marvin Rice. He's from Memphis. When I tried to interview him he was so excited about his trip to Japan that he wouldn't talk, but took a card from his pocketbook, handed it to me and hurried away."

"Yes?"

"The only thing on the card was a line written in ink that said, *'Remember January 15, 1921.'* "

Next morning about two hours before sailing time, I followed Miss Gaw's tip and looked Rice up. I found him on deck and asked what the card meant. He seemed startled, went through his pocketbook, and said:

"I gave Miss Gaw the wrong card. I meant to give her my business card. I always keep this one as a reminder of a very important day in my life."

"Sounds like a story," I said.

"Yes, it is a story," Rice agreed. "On that date, God showed me how to become successful and happy in business." He smiled wryly. "I'm sort of an inquisitive person. At school, kids called me 'Nosy.' I'm still nosy, but that card helps me remember to mind my own business."

He started to turn away, but I invited him to go down to the lounge with me for tea. There, amid the hurry and scurry of a ship about to sail, Rice talked.

"I left home when I was twelve," he said, "and I never saw my father again. But he willed me a thriving hay, grain and feed business. My father had had lots of customers, and the respect of every merchant along the street. Three months after I took over, business began to drop. Old customers fell off. New ones didn't stay. Within a year the business was barely breaking even. At the end of the second year, I knew bankruptcy was only weeks away.

"I had one customer who'd stayed with me all along. He was a retired college professor named John Robinson, and he raised chickens as a hobby. He was a crotchety old fellow who spoke his mind. He asked, one day, 'Have you read Horace?'

" 'Horace, who?' I asked.

" 'Quintus Horatius Flaccus. He died about eight years before Jesus was born.'

" 'No, I'm too busy to read,' I told him. 'This business is going downhill fast.'

"Professor Robinson snorted. 'Too busy doing what?'

" 'Well,' I said, 'I'm busy at lots of things. I like to help people. When I see folks making mistakes, I point out the right way. Take your chickens, now. Professor. You shouldn't have gone in for Plymouth Rocks. They're a good breed, all right, but some of the newer breeds . . .'

" 'Rubbish,' the old fellow snapped. He picked up his package of cracked wheat and stomped out.

"I said to Gus, my colored helper: 'That's the way it is with people you try to help. They don't appreciate it.'

" 'Yes, sir,' Gus said.

" 'Take Milandy, the furniture man,' I said. 'He bought all that new-style stock of furniture. I told him time and again that that would be a mistake. Would he listen? No!'

" 'Guess he lost a lot of money on that deal, too,' Gus said.

" 'Well, no,' I admitted, 'he didn't lose. He made a quick profit. But that's not the idea. He should have known that a new line like that is a gamble in this territory. This is an old, conservative community, and . . .'

" 'Boss,' Gus interrupted, 'I gotta get to work. We keep

talking so much sometimes I just can't seem to catch up.'
Gus backed off, but I said:

"'Just a minute, Gus. I hear you're going to have another
baby at your house. That's too bad. You've got seven kids
now. How do you keep them all eating?'

"'Sally and me loves babies, Boss. We just got to have
new babies from time to time. We's got so much love inside
us we just has to have more kids to love. We eats all right.'

"'Well,' I said, 'everybody loves babies, but even so . . .'

"'Boss, *please*, I gotta get to work. I gotta take care of
things around here.'

"'Okay,' I said, 'take care of things. I've got to go see
George Schneider, anyway. Hear he's enlarging his store.'

"'Boss,' Gus said, 'maybe you better stay here and help
me. I can use some help.'

"Gus often annoyed me, but he was a hard worker, and he
meant well. He did need help with the work, but business
was so poor that I couldn't afford another hand.

"In November 1920, wholesalers began bearing down on
me. Bills were long overdue, and collection letters were de-
manding. At about that same time, Gus's eighth baby was
born, and Gus asked for a raise.

"I said, 'Gus, I warned you about so many babies. I'm
sorry things are tough at your house, but I can't give you
a raise. The business just won't stand it.' Then, ashamed of
my harshness, I asked: 'You folks eating all right, Gus?'

"'Yes, sir. God sees we don't go hungry, but we sure do a
powerful lot of praying. Sally and me feels you're goin' to
give me that raise, Boss, 'cause we prayed so hard. And, Boss,
with you gallivantin' so much, I sure enough earn it. I work
hard around here.'

"Well, of course, Gus got his raise. A few more dollars
going out wouldn't make much difference.

"I was a regular church member, and gave lots of my time

advising and helping our board and officials, but I'd never been much of a hand to pray. Gus had got me thinking a good deal about prayer, now.

" 'When you pray, Gus,' I asked, 'what do you ask God for? Food? Clothes?'

"Gus looked surprised. 'Why no, Boss. We don't ask God for things like that. We don't think we knows enough to tell God what to give us. We just says: "God, we're doin' the best we knows how, but sometimes it don't seem like we're doin' enough. Please, will You just keep right on helpin' us like You been doin'? And thank You, God." '

"I turned away. I *knew* what *I* needed. And I knew what I wanted. Right now, I wanted a miracle to save my business.

"That was in November. All the rest of that month, and all through December, I watched my business grow worse. Creditors stopped being polite. They threatened. And throughout those dark days, I couldn't get Gus's simple philosophy of prayer out of my mind. Early in January, my creditors got together and filed joint suit against me. Trial date was January 27.

"To me, bankruptcy seemed about the worst disgrace a man could endure. And for *me* to go broke was particularly humiliating, for I'd been advising other merchants along the street for two years. And most of them were doing well— even the ones who'd ignored my ideas and suggestions.

"Came a morning when in desperation, I said to Gus: 'If you had this business and saw it going broke, Gus, how would you pray?'

" 'Well, Boss—if I had a cord of wood to chop, and didn't feel up to it, I'd ask God to give me strength for the job. And then, I'd get in and chop.'

" 'I'm afraid it's too late for that,' I said. 'Thanks any-way, Gus.'

"Then came the day I prayed—January 15. I was so distressed and uncertain of myself that morning that over and over, I repeated: 'God, please show me what to do. I've tried to be helpful to others. I've tried to be a good neighbor, but something's wrong. I don't know what to do, God.'

"About noon, Professor Robinson came in, ordered some laying mash, and said, 'You look troubled, Rice. Anything I can do?'

"Suddenly I was pouring out my heart to him. I told how I dreaded the disgrace of bankruptcy; how although I'd spent much time trying to help my fellow merchants, now that I was in need of money, none would lend to me.

" 'This was a thriving business when I took over,' I said, 'but customers began quitting almost at once. Today, Professor, you're about the only customer my father had, who's still buying here. Why didn't you quit like the others?'

" 'Because you sell good merchandise, Rice. Anyway, I liked your father very much. You don't have to go broke, you know.'

" 'Well,' I said, 'I've tried everything—even prayer.'

"The professor's face brightened. 'Well, maybe you're ready now for the truth, Rice. Maybe you can listen without being so cocksure about everything.'

" 'I don't feel cocksure about anything,' I said. 'I'm desperate, Professor.'

"The old man took off his glasses, laid them on the counter and said: 'Some time ago I asked you if you'd read Horace. You replied, I think, that you'd been too busy to read.'

" 'That's right. I remember.'

" 'You've been so busy advising others, Rice, that you've had no time for your own business. Right?'

" 'That's right.'

" 'Horace said, almost two thousand years ago, *"I attend to the business of other people, having lost my own."* '

" 'But . . .' I began.

"Professor Robinson went on: 'Another old Roman, who lived years before Horace, said: *"Have you so much leisure from your own business that you can take care of other people's that does not at all belong to you?"* '

" 'But . . .'

" 'No buts. Your business has run down because you've been so busy minding other people's business that you've had no time to mind your own. Stop it. You're a man with a feeling of inferiority. You've been trying to compensate for that by trying to show others how smart you are. In the eyes of other merchants, you're a fool. Don't you realize that they know what a mess your business is in? You bore them. You bore your customers.'

"He picked up his glasses, perched them on the tip of his nose, peered over them and said, 'Well?'

" 'I feel sick, Professor,' I said. I turned and walked blindly to my office. After a long time, I called Gus.

" 'Gus,' I asked, 'tell me honestly: Do you think it's my fault that my business is on the rocks?'

"Gus said, 'Boss, it ain't for me to tell you such things, but there ain't nothing wrong with the business, so it must be you. Your father used to say this business belonged to God. He said God grew the hay, the grain and the oats. Your father told me God was just lettin' him sell those things so he could be happy and have plenty. Your father even wrote it in a book.'

" 'What book?'

" 'That little old dusty notebook you put in the catchall closet when you first came.'

"I found the notebook in a pile of old papers and ledgers. I opened it, and on the very first page, my father had written:

"Maltbie Babcock says that the world is God's workshop; the raw materials are His; the ideals and patterns are His; our hands are 'members of Christ,' our reward His recognition. Blacksmith or banker, draughtsman or doctor, painter or preacher, servant or statesman, must work as unto the Lord, not merely making a living, but devoting a life. This makes life sacramental, turning its water into wine. This is twice blessed, blessing both the worker and the work.

"When I put down the notebook, I knew what I must do. I asked that a special creditors' meeting be called. At that meeting, I told my story just as I've told it to you. The creditors said they were for me, and would do all they could to help me regain what I'd lost through neglect.

"One of the creditors said: 'Running a business for God should make a man mighty proud. Makes a man work hard so God can be proud of him.'

"I figured it'd take a year or more to get square with the world, but it didn't. It took about seven months. I don't lose customers any more; and I sure don't nose into things that don't concern me. The way I see it, Gus was right when he said there was nothing wrong with the business—only with me. Once I got straightened out, success came naturally. There can't be any business failure for the man who manages a business for God."

IN 1935 I asked fifty physicians chosen at random from the Los Angeles telephone directory, if they believed that spiritual healings—that is—physical and mental healings by faith alone, were possible.

Twenty-seven said: "Yes."

Eleven said: "I don't know."

Twelve said: "No."

Again in June 1955, I asked the same question of fifty Los Angeles doctors.

Forty-seven said: "Yes."

One said: "I don't know."

Two said: "No."

Three of the twelve who'd said "No" in 1935, said "Yes" in 1955. When I asked what had happened to change their minds, the three said, in effect:

"We have learned that Man's natural state is one of well-being; and that there is a spiritual entity in Man that when activated by faith, destroys physical and mental illness."

That statement means, of course, that if one has faith, there are almost no incurable diseases. If, as these physicians state, the natural state of man is well-being, then financial, and other forms of insecurity, are also "diseases" that also can be cured by faith.

George Muller, who kept a life-long record of his prayers and their answers—twenty-five thousand of them—many of them miraculous, says:

"Prayer is the source of faith, and faith accomplishes all good things."

They Keep Books on Prayer

ON THE MORNING of Sunday, April 8, 1951, William McCormick, a businessman of San Jose, California, did something he'd done several times before. He gave the last of his savings to a friend in need, then went home and prayed.

On his desk was a ledger on the cover of which was written: "If ye shall ask anything in my name, that will I do." In the ledger, he made this entry:

"April 8, 11 A.M. Prayed God to direct me to a business that I can buy with no down-payment."

On April 14, six days later, McCormick made another entry:

"Prayer of April 8 answered today. I dropped into one of the best-equipped dry-cleaning establishments in the city, and told the proprietor I'd owned several successful dry-cleaning businesses in my time, and that I was looking for another one to buy. After we talked a while, he said he might be interested in selling, as he'd made a lot of money and would like to retire. I told him I had no money for a down-payment. He said he didn't particularly care for a down-payment; that he thought I was a good man, and that I could pay him out of earnings. We made the deal. Total cost will be $22,000."

That was on Saturday. On Monday, April 16, after necessary papers were signed, McCormick took over the plant.

That same Monday morning, Richard Nolan, a Campbell,

California, floriculturist, and a friend of McCormick's, made an entry in a similar ledger. It read:

"Final proof that God answered my prayer of December 1, 1949, was given today when my new tetraploid Easter lily bloomed. Its flowers are almost twice as large as the ordinary lily, and stems and leaves are much sturdier than I'd hoped for. From this plant, I can now propagate a giant lily equal to, or better than, the one developed recently at the U.S. Agricultural Experimental Station at Beltsville, Maryland."

After reading this entry, I asked Nolan: "What is a tetraploid lily?"

"The bulblets of a normal lily," Nolan said, "have a chromosome count of twenty-four. Such lilies are called diploids. If you 'shock' those bulblets with radio-activity, or with a drug called colchicine, the resulting plants sometimes have a chromosome count of thirty-six, and are called tetraploids. That means that the flowers, leaves, stems—the whole plant —will be at least one-third larger than its parents.

"The shock treatment with colchicine is simple. A lily bulb is made up of scales, something like the cloves of garlic. You soak these scales in a .2 per cent solution of colchicine for 150 minutes, then plant them in flats. Tiny bulblets will develop on most of the scales. Some of these bulblets will appear normal. Others will appear 'different.'

"Plant the 'different' bulblets, still attached to the scale, about two inches deep in your garden. The resulting plants will be larger than normal ones. Some will be freakish. But a few, perhaps one in two hundred, will develop into perfect giant lilies. Often the first year's flowers will show little improvement over the parent plants; but plant the bulblets from them the following year, and results will astonish and please you. You will sense more than ever, your partnership with God—for with His help, you've created a new variety.

"Well, back in December, 1949, I treated about a thousand scales with colchicine. I figured that about five of these scales would prove to be perfect tetraploids. I planted the thousand in one large flat and placed it under a tree where it would be shaded much of the time. As I always do with my flowers, I prayed that God would give them His loving care.

"The treated scales sprouted. All looked healthy and vigorous. Then, a neighbor's cow broke through my fence and trampled the flat into a mess. At first I thought every scale was destroyed, but I salvaged twelve that seemed uninjured.

" 'God,' I said, 'the mathematical chance of getting a perfect tetraploid lily out of twelve scales is pretty thin. But I believe that a perfect new lily is among these rescued twelve.' "

It was!

Nolan took me out to his greenhouse and showed me those lily plants. Nine of the twelve were normal. Two were freaks. But the twelfth had the most perfect tetraploid Easter lily blooms imaginable: flowers twelve-and-a-half inches long, petals pure white and velvety, and a fragrance sweeter than incense.

I invited McCormick and Nolan to my home one evening to tell me more about this business of keeping records of prayers, and their answers. They came, bringing with them a Seattle building-material wholesaler named Wilbur Dawson, who also kept prayer records. Dawson said:

"Prayer records are kept by thousands of Christians. I believe a businessman should keep just as accurate records of his prayers, as he does of his financial condition. I believe— and so do Nolan, and McCormick—that prayer is the cornerstone of successful business."

"I've proved that over and over," McCormick said. "Several times, I've taken over dry-cleaning businesses that seemed hopeless—businesses loaded with debts and unsavory reputations. With God's help, advice and encouragement, I built them into successful businesses."

"George Muller's life," Nolan said, "convinced us that we should keep records of our prayers."

"Who's George Muller?" I asked.

"George Muller," Dawson said, "was a famous English preacher and philanthropist—and a good businessman. Muller preached—and proved—that man's temporal, as well as spiritual, needs can be supplied by prayer.

"He wrote in his journal: 'During my lifetime I have had twenty-five thousand prayers answered—and five thousand of these answers came on the very day I made the petitions."

"Muller devoted most of his life to the care of orphan children," McCormick said. "A poor man, he started his work by taking only a few children into his home. He lodged, clothed and fed them. At the peak of his activities, he was caring for more than two thousand youngsters, and had built five houses to shelter them. He met his heavy expenses through prayer. Never once did he advertise, solicit, or ask men for funds."

"And so far as is known," Nolan added, "no child in his care ever missed a meal through lack of food, or was ever cold for lack of clothes."

"One morning," said Dawson, "Muller was told by despondent cooks that there was no food to feed two thousand hungry youngsters. The night before, they'd dusted the flour barrels, and had used the last crumb from the pantries. The prospect of breakfast seemed so hopeless that they'd not even built the fires in the kitchen stoves.

"George Muller said: 'Go start the fires and put on the kettles as if there were an abundance of food—and there will be.'

"He said: 'Listen: *"I have been young, and now am old;*

*Yet have I not seen the righteous forsaken, Nor his seed beg-
ging bread." '*

"And then Muller went to his room, locked the door, and
prayed. In a short time, two food-laden wagons arrived from
opposite directions—and two thousand children were fed."

"That must be the same George Muller," I said, "who
made a preaching tour of Europe, America, India, Australia,
and China back in the 'eighties and 'nineties."

"Yes," Nolan said, "that's the same man. He started that
tour when he was past seventy, and continued it for seventeen years. Muller proved in his own life, that prayer is the
open door to God's direction of every decent human activity."

"Just how does keeping prayer records help?" I asked.
"Why not just pray, and forget it?"

All three men started to answer, but Nolan and Dawson
let McCormick explain. He said:

"Well, the act of writing out your prayers eliminates
those that are foolish or unnecessary. It also helps you avoid
'vain repetitions.'

"The answers—written down in black and white—are a
constant reminder of the love of God, and your need of Him
in all your undertakings.

"A prayer record book, handed to a man whose doubts
have kept him from contacting God as the source of all good,
helps build his faith in a way that few other things do.

"There are many other reasons why we believe that records of prayers should be kept, but I think the chief good
of such records is that they're a permanent testimony to the
truth of Christ's promise:

" 'Ask, and it shall be given you; seek, and ye shall find;
knock, and it shall be opened unto you.' "

THE ONLY time I've been in Dr. Rab Lindsey's private office was when I took the manuscript of "I Dressed Them, and God Healed Them" to him for his approval. While he read the manuscript, I studied the diplomas and pictures on his walls. Among them, neatly framed, were these two quotations:

PRAYER

More things are wrought by prayer
Than this world dreams of. Wherefore, let thy voice
Rise like a fountain for me night and day.
For what are men better than sheep or goats
That nourish a blind life within the brain
If, knowing God, they lift not hands of prayer
Both for themselves and those who call them friend?
For so the whole round earth is every way
Bound by gold chains about the feet of God.

—*Alfred, Lord Tennyson*
(*From* Idylls of the King)

Arise, then, freeman, stand forth in thy world. It is God's world. It is therefore thine.

—*Joshua Royce*
(*From* The World and the Individual)

I Dressed Them and God Healed Them

I CAME OUT OF anesthesia, vaguely aware that I was lying on a bed in a San Francisco veterans' hospital. A voice had wakened me, and I looked around the room to find its source. It had been a man's voice, saying triumphantly:

"Paré! Ambroise Paré! That's the name!"

Then I smiled weakly, realizing that the voice had been my own. Gray mist seemed to invade the room as I passed back into anesthesia again.

When I wakened next time, Dr. Rab Lindsey, the surgeon who'd operated, was bending over me.

"Doctor," I said, "when you prayed this morning just before operating on me, I wanted to tell you that you reminded me of Dr. Ambroise Paré—head army surgeon for Colonel Montejan about the year 1545."

Dr. Lindsey smiled. "Paré's the doctor who always said: 'I dressed them, and God healed them,' isn't he? That word 'dressed,' of course, meant 'treated' or 'operated.' 'I *operated* on them, and God healed them.'"

"Soldiers' wounds were terrible in those days," I said. "Great holes torn by pikes, swords, round shot . . ."

"Don't talk any more now," Dr. Lindsey said. "Rest awhile. The nurse will stay close by."

"Have you always prayed before operations, Doctor?" I asked.

215

"No—not always. As a young doctor, I was too brash to pray."

"The anesthetist also prayed this morning."

"That's right. Now, *please* don't talk any more."

"I collect prayer stories, Doctor," I said.

"Well, later, if you wish, you may have mine to add to your collection," Dr. Lindsey said, *"if* you'll try to sleep now."

TWO WEEKS LATER, when I was nearly back to normal health, Dr. Lindsey told me the following story:

"I AM SCOTS-CANADIAN—the eldest of nine children born on a forty-acre farm that my grandfather cleared in the forest. Our days at home began and ended with family prayer, and a short discourse on a Bible text by my father, who'd shut his eyes, open the Bible at random and put his finger on a verse.

"Father's discipline was rigorous. At four each morning—winter and summer—I'd start milking our five cows. At five, I'd feed the horses. At five-thirty I'd clean the stables. At six, I'd wash for breakfast. After breakfast I'd strain the milk, pour it into wide, shallow pans and set the pans in a wooden tank in the milk house. In summer, that tank ran an inch deep with water from a cool, deep well.

"At eight o'clock I'd begin the three-mile walk to a small country school, carrying a lard pail that always contained two thick slices of meat between equally thick slices of home-made bread, an apple, and a slab of apple pie. I was always so hungry that I'd eat half my lunch at morning recess, and the remainder at noon. By afternoon recess I'd feel starved, and could hardly wait to get home and devour four or five slices of bread and butter before beginning the evening chores.

"My younger brothers and sisters worked hard at their chores, too. And Father never seemed to rest, but it was Mother who worked hardest of all of us. Mother's world was made up of the kitchen, pantry, milk house and buttery. She was a tiny Scots lady with a Highland accent, and when I was a wee lad, she'd tell me stories as I followed her about from kitchen stove to sink, to pantry, to buttery. That large, cool, sweet-smelling buttery was really my mother's prayer room. There on her knees, she found strength to do work too hard for so frail a body.

"That buttery! It was a lean-to built against the shaded side of the house. The room was about fifteen feet long and twelve feet wide. There were no windows on the three sides lined with shelves, but the top half of the north side held a row of small-paned windows which Mother kept frosted with occasional coats of thin whitewash. And under the windows was a long, strong, oak table.

"Each year by the time the first snow fell, the table and shelves were loaded with glass jars containing what Mother called 'goodies'—watermelon preserves with cinnamon sticks showing through, spiced plums, crabapples in syrup, apple butter, green beans sliced in thin strings, green peas with a slice of onion buried in them, dried peas ground into flour, and corn put up in milk. There were wild berries and fruits—strawberries, blackberries, blueberries, choke-cherries, elderberries. There were rows of jellies so clear and bright that the glasses seemed made of garnet, ruby and amber.

"And there were other things in that buttery—food was always plentiful in Father's house. There were candied orange peel, eggs in water-glass, wild honey, headcheese, hams, sides of bacon, pickles, ketchup . . ." Dr. Lindsey paused.

"And God was there, too," he added.

"And our clothes—made from cloth woven by Mother and my sisters—were strong and warm, as were our heavy, knitted socks, sweaters, mittens, and the winter 'chukes' that snuggled our heads and ears, and hung jauntily down our backs with yarn tassels at the ends. Homemade quilts and comforters on our featherbeds kept us snug and warm through coldest winter nights.

"Money, though, was scarce. It required four years of saving by the whole family, to accumulate the one hundred dollars with which I started off to college to become a doctor —a momentous day!

"All of us children had gone through measles, mumps, tonsillitis, diphtheria, and various fevers, without a doctor— for the nearest doctor was ninety miles away. Kind neighbors had acted as doctor, nurse or midwife in our home. But always, there was apprehension that someday a life might depend upon a doctor—and there'd be no doctor.

"So, even before I was a schoolboy, it was decided that I was to go away to college, learn the mysteries of the medical profession, and return home to work among the people of our backwoods community.

"I dreamed often, while a lad, of my triumphant return. I'd be sophisticated and learned, and carry a satchel filled with instruments, pills and small bottles. Neighbors and friends would call me 'Doctor,' and I'd feel happy and proud. And when that day came, my mother would wear a lavender dress and a neat, gray bonnet. My father would wear a long-tailed black coat when he went to church, and I'd send all my brothers and sisters to fine, suitable schools.

"On the evening before I left for college, Father brought his 'money-sock' from the battered, leather trunk in his bedroom, and while the family sat wide-eyed in a circle of lamplight, he up-ended the sock and poured out on the table the

savings of four years—$100.44. Thoughtfully, he pushed the
hundred dollars into a pile, picked up the forty-four cents,
and dropped them back into the sock. Then he put the hundred dollars—in coins and small bills—into a homemade
leather pouch, drew the drawstring and handed the pouch to
me. He said:

" 'It's the family that's sending ye off to college, Rab, and
we're verra happy knowing that your education belongs to
all of us. We'll miss your help on the farm, and we'll be able
to send ye verra little money. So be prudent, Rabbie. Ye'll
no doubt find a job to help ye through.'

"My father's stern face showed nothing of his feelings, but
that name, 'Rabbie,' brought tears to my eyes. The last time
he'd called me 'Rabbie' had been when I was a wee fellow,
very ill with scarlet fever. The neighbor-woman who'd
helped nurse me had told Father she thought I was dying.

"Father'd lifted my hand and said huskily, 'Rabbie, Rabbie
—must ye go?'

"And now, again, he'd called me 'Rabbie.'

"Next morning as I stood beside the buckboard in which
my brother, Donald, was to drive me to the railway, Mother
whispered, 'Your-r mither will be bein' pr-roud, Rab, laddie.'

"My eyes followed her as she walked away. I knew she was
going to the buttery to give me into the care of God.

"Until late that afternoon, when I'd gotten into the train
and had waved goodbye to Donald, I'd felt well-dressed and
comfortable in my best homespun suit. But amused stares of
passengers soon made me feel a very gawk. By the time I got
to Toronto, I felt so awkward and humiliated that I was
stumbling over my feet. I couldn't endure that, so went into
the first clothing store I saw and bought a suit, shirt, hat
and shoes.

"Then, with a large part of my hundred dollars spent, I

went looking for a job. I found one within two blocks of
the depot—dishwasher in an armchair restaurant—night work
at nine dollars a week, and meals.

"In college, finding I could stay near the top in all of my
classes, I soon became self-assured—even cocky. I had visions
of a medical practice among the wealthy in some large city—
preferably, New York. I even began calling my father's
farm, 'Our country place.' By the end of the fourth year, my
ego'd become so inflated that I no longer felt the need of
God's help.

"Later, in medical school, after one of my professors told
me I was destined to be a great surgeon, I began thinking
of myself as an atheist. During discussions with student
friends, I'd hold forth at great length on 'superstitious religious beliefs.' Belief in God was a fine thing for the timid,
the ignorant and the inept, I maintained, but the strong man
—the deep man—the thinking man—that man was his own
God.

"And so it was throughout my internship. And so it was
during my first years of practice. Success came quickly, for I
was a good surgeon. A grateful American woman patient
staked me to plush offices in a large American city. And she
introduced me to moneyed friends.

"I didn't let my family know I wasn't going home to do
doctoring until after I'd begun my American practice.
Mother's response to my decision touched me deeply. She
wrote:

> "The news that ye're no comin' home has left Father
> and all, fair fashed. It is your life to live, Rab, but
> mind, laddie, that ye always let God's love guard ye.

"Dear, gentle heart—my mother.

"My American practice was successful from the start. I

undertook general surgery, and soon built a reputation as an able man. I sent money home from time to time, hoping it would help send my brothers and sisters to college, and it wasn't until much later that I learned that every penny had been saved, 'against the time that God'd be sendin' ye back to your ain folk to doctor amang them, and ye'd be needin' th' money for medicines and all.'

"Two years followed in which almost everything I undertook turned out right. Operations that had seemed hopeless, resulted in cures. Fees mounted, of course, as more and more wealthy people came to me, and eventually I repaid the borrowed money that had financed my offices and equipment. I knew I was spoken of as a coming man, in medical circles, and I felt self-assured—even smug.

"Then shortly after the beginning of my third year of practice came a series of shocks. In one week, I lost two patients because of unforeseen complications following their operations. The following week, I looked up from my desk one afternoon and saw what I thought for a moment must be a ghost—a man named Chapman. Nine months earlier, I'd told Chapman that he had no chance to live. I'd said to him kindly:

" 'Your malignancy has gone too far, Chapman. Surgery can't help you—nothing can help you.'

" 'How long do I have, Doctor?' he'd asked.

" 'Three months, Chapman—four at the most,' I'd answered.

"And there was Chapman standing in front of me nine months later—obviously a well man. My hands trembled.

"Chapman grinned. 'Fooled you, Doctor,' he said. 'Thought you should know that there *was* help for me.' He pulled up a chair and sat down. 'I've just had a check-up by a group of doctors,' he said. 'God—prayer has made me well.'

"I sat and stared at him. He went on:

" 'You know, Doctor—". . . the prayer of faith shall save the sick, and the Lord will raise him up . . . [James 5:15]." '

" 'Tell me about it, Chapman,' I said.

" 'Well, after I left here that day you pronounced my death sentence, I didn't *feel* like a condemned man. Instead, I felt anger against the evil trying to kill me. I'd not really prayed for years, but that day as I walked the street, I found myself repeating a Bible verse I'd learned as a boy: *Thou shalt not be afraid for the terror by night; nor for the arrow that flieth by day; Nor for the pestilence that walketh in darkness; nor for the destruction that wasteth at noonday.* [Psalms 91:5-6]

" 'When I noticed an Episcopalian church on my way home, I entered it to rest and to think. In the pew where I sat was part of a pamphlet—a report by the Chicago Committee of The Commission on Religion and Health of the Federal Council of Churches. It told results of an investigation of spiritual healings. The Committee consisted of Dr. Charles S. Braden, professor of History and Literature of Religions, Northwestern University; Dr. Carrol A. Wise, of Garrett Biblical Institute; and Dr. W. E. Blakemore, of the University of Chicago. The report said that questionnaires had been sent to one thousand clergymen, and that those who'd returned them had reported a total of sixty-four kinds of disease that had been cured by faith in God. There were several kinds of cancer—cancer of the lungs, the spine, the mouth, the duodenum, the bone, and in addition, ten unspecified kinds. The report said that in nearly every case, diagnosis had been made by a competent doctor, and there'd been medical attendance for a long, or a short period.

" 'I read one case reported, over and over, Doctor,' Chapman continued. 'It was cancer, diagnosed and treated by a doctor who pronounced it hopeless of cure. Within one month—due to prayer—that patient was well enough to go home. Within six months, she was doing her housework. Four years later, medical examination showed she was still completely healed.

" 'Another case, reported by a Methodist minister, told of a patient whose illness had been diagnosed as lung cancer by a group of physicians in consultation. The patient was given *one week* to live. Her minister prayed for her; she made herself right with God; the next day, she began to improve. Two years later she was still well.

" 'There were other kinds of spiritual healings reported— permanent cures of heart disease, paralysis, tuberculosis, polio, arthritis, and other ailments.

" 'Well, Doctor, after I'd finished reading that report, I sat a long while, looking at a stained-glass window with the sunlight shining through it. I thought back over my life. I'd committed no crimes, but I'd been a hearty hater of those whom I'd thought had wronged me. I'd never taken revengeful *action* against any, but I'd cherished *thoughts* of revenge. Sitting there looking Death in the face, I realized my great sin was that the good I might have done—I'd left undone. "Forgive me, God, for having been one of Life's slackers," I said. At once, I experienced an inpouring of faith, and a surge of hope.

" 'I don't really know how long I sat, recalling Bible texts I'd learned in Sunday school. And one I remembered with new understanding, strongly lifted my spirit: *But unto you that fear my Name shall the Son of righteousness arise with healing in His wings.* [Malachi 4:2]

" 'The sun was setting as I left the church. I then went to my own minister, and asked him to pray with me.

" 'That was almost nine months ago,' he said.

"AFTER CHAPMAN HAD gone," Dr. Lindsey continued, "I sat trying to find some 'scientific' or 'psychological' reason for his cure. I found none. A week later I still had no satisfactory answer. I'd probably have tried to shrug the thing off as an unsolvable mystery had I not met a woman who showed me her medical history, signed by physicians of good repute. She'd been another 'hopeless' case—a heart condition. She'd been completely healed at the Catholic shrine at Lourdes, France.

"The 'cures' at Lourdes, and similar shrines, I'd believed, were hysterical psychological reactions, and could not possibily be termed real healings. I decided to find out the truth, once for all.

"I visited Lourdes, to observe in the light of 'cold reason.' My first surprise was to learn that more than 1,600 investigating doctors from all parts of the world had visited Lourdes during the preceding twelve months. Then I learned that cures claimed as miracles by the Official Bureau of Church and State had been thoroughly investigated over a period of years, and that the findings were backed by prolonged medical checking.

"I found that all claims of miracles that might be associated with psychological factors, were disallowed, and that to be accepted as a miracle, a case must have met these conditions:

" (1) The time factor of the cure must have been much shorter than would normally have been the case.

" (2) There must never have been a relapse.

" (3) The cure must have been under observation for several years.

" (4) The clinical features of the ailment which had existed at the time of the cure must have been entirely removed.

"Before I sailed for home, I met with nine other investigating physicians—Protestants—and we went into every phase of Lourdes' healings. The cures declared 'miracles' by the

Official Bureau, we agreed, were undoubtedly miraculous. But we also agreed that thousands of cures *not* certified as 'miracles' were genuine, nonetheless.

"The other nine doctors were happy to have proved that spiritual healings were possible, but I was dejected. I'd been compelled—by the evidence—to admit that God lived, and was able and willing to aid, comfort and heal. But that admission was not enough to lift the burden of guilt I felt because of my years of atheism. How many persons had I harmed, I wondered, by my ignorant assertions? How many were even now struggling in despondency because I'd encouraged or taught them to doubt?

"Back in America, I questioned religious leaders of all denominations—ministers, rabbis, priests. Many told me they prayed for bodies as well as for souls.

"I also discussed prayer with several highly competent physicians and surgeons, and learned with something of a shock that most combined prayer with their medical and their surgical techniques.

"I became more and more troubled. How was it I'd gone so long without learning that prayer was part of the healing practice of doctors and surgeons? How was it I'd not been aware that men of all faiths prayed, and received answers? I concluded I'd been so overwhelmed by my own 'importance' that I'd not been interested in what others might believe.

"On my knees, I admitted my fault. I prayed many times, but always rose from my knees with a feeling that some fault still within me kept God from answering.

"One day while discussing my problem with Dr. Clyde Randolph, a minister versed in philosophy and literature, I burst out, 'After all, is it so strange that *I* should have denied the existence of God when so many great scientists and philosophers have been atheists?'

"Dr. Randolph looked a bit surprised, and said:

" 'Some scientific and philosophical leaders have been agnostics in their early days, but off-hand, I can't think of any who remained unbelievers after they matured. To which ones are you referring?'

"I thought for a moment, then said, 'I'm not certain, but it seems to me that Einstein . . .' I paused, questioningly.

" 'Go on,' Dr. Randolph said.

" 'Well, Einstein, Voltaire, Spinoza, the early Greeks, the psychologists . . . I can't remember all of them, but I've heard, and I've read . . .'

" 'Do you read a lot?'

" 'I've never had time to read very much besides medicine, but it seems to me that if *great* thinkers couldn't believe . . .'

" 'You should begin to do some serious reading, Dr. Lindsey,' he said, 'because you don't really know what you're talking about. Einstein, Spinoza, Voltaire, and many of the Greeks, and many psychologists, believed in God, and said so. Einstein—the scientist who reached farther into the stretches of the universe than any other man who ever lived —summed up his life's work by saying that his researches had led him to the belief that all was created and controlled by a Supreme Being. He called that Supreme Being "God," for in discussing the orderliness of universal laws, Einstein wrote that he did not believe that God played at dice with men.

" 'Voltaire, in *La Henriada*,' Dr. Randolph went on, 'said: "God has made thee to love Him . . ." ' But read for yourself, Lindsey. And stop thinking of yourself as a great man. Instead, think of yourself as God's man.'

"My associate in practice was getting along quite well without me, so I extended my vacation, and undertook some intensive reading. I read Cicero: 'The celestial order and beauty of the universe compel me to admit that there is some excellent and eternal Being, who deserves the respect and homage of men.' [1] And Ovid: 'Nothing is so lofty or so far above danger that it is not below and in the power of God.' [2] and Plautus: 'There is indeed a God that sees and hears whate'er we do.' [3] And Pindar: 'If any man hopes, in whatever he does, to escape the eye of God, he is grievously wrong.' [4]

"I read Spinoza: '. . . the love of God for men and the mind's intellectual love towards God is one and the same thing. From this we clearly understand in what consists our salvation, or liberty, namely, in the constant and eternal love for God, or in the love of God for men.'

"My reading continued. I learned that almost every great student came, in time, to believe in a God that ruled the universe—and ruled with love. I took up the works of psychologists. I'd assumed all psychologists were atheistic—probably because Freud wrote mostly of man's evil side. I read C. G. Jung, often called the greatest psychologist of all. He wrote: 'The truly religious person . . . knows that God has brought all sorts of strange and inconceivable things to pass, and seeks in the most curious ways to enter a man's heart. He therefore senses in everything the unseen presence of the divine will.' And again: '. . . if the Doctor wishes to help a human being, he must accept him as he is. And he can do this in reality only when he has already seen and accepted himself as he is.' And again: 'Healing may be called a religious problem.'

"In short," Lindsey said, "the books showed me that a *little* philosophy is indeed a dangerous thing. It makes callow minds impudent. On the other hand, profundity in philosophy invariably leads to God. As an example, Benjamin

[1] *De Divinatione,* Bk. II, ch. 72, sec. 148.
[2] *Tristia,* Bk. IV, eleg. 8, 1. 47.
[3] *Captivi,* 1. 313. (Act ii, sc. 2)
[4] *Olympian Odes,* Ode i, 1. 64.

Franklin, when mentally an unfeathered fledgling, loudly voiced doubts that God existed, but when nis mind acquired the feathers of maturity, he wrote:

" 'God governs in the affairs of men; and if a sparrow cannot fall to the ground without His notice, neither can a kingdom rise without His aid.'

"And so, on my knees, I abandoned immature thinking—realized and acknowledged that whatever talents and capacities I had, came from God. I undertook to live thereafter not as my own man, but as God's man.

"I was now eager to resume practice, and would have done so the following day except for a telegram which arrived from my brother, Donald:

> *"Doctor says Mother has only a few days to live. Come quickly. I'll bide in Guelph until you get here.*

"The telephone company located Donald for me at an inexpensive hotel.

" 'What's ailing Mother, Donald?' I asked.

" 'A new doctor lives among us now,' Donald said. 'He offers no hope. Come away home, Rab boy.'

" 'But answer me, Donald. What's the matter with Mother?'

" 'She was gored in the chest by yon crooked-horned Jersey. There's complications. Mither says nought about pain, but she suffers, Rabbie, and I canna stand it.' His voice broke.

" 'Buck up, man,' I said. 'Is yon doctor a surgeon?'

" 'He's just a lad new frae school.'

" 'I'll hire a plane, Donald,' I said. 'We should make the landing field at Guelph before daybreak.'

"I called Dr. McLeod, my anesthetist, told him to bring what was necessary and to meet me at the airport, then called my nurse, Mrs. McLean, told her to meet me at the office prepared to accompany Dr. McLeod and me, and to pack the special drugs and instruments I might need.

"At sunrise, when the plane landed at Guelph, Donald was waiting with an old, battered Ford. Four hours and two blowouts later, we chugged to a stop before our old, log barn. Father took my hand as I stepped stiffly from the car, and said:

" 'Hame at last, Rabbie, eh?'

"As we walked together to the house, Father said, 'Th' young doctor-r has stayed wi' Mither-r nicht an' day. He thinks ther-re's no hope. But it's not yet th' thr-ree scor-re year-rs an' ten f'r Mither-r, pr-romised by th' Bible, Rabbie, so wi' y'r fine doctor-rin' it may be that ye'll save her-r to us. Eh, Rabbie?'

" 'Donald mentioned complications, Father,' I said, 'but he didn't seem to know what.'

" 'Th' young doctor-r says th' cow's hor-rn br-roke off a bit of a r-rib an' pushed it into th' lung. That's one com-pleecation. But th' other-r compleecation is Mither-r, her-rsel', Rab. She wor-rked her-rsel' into a gr-reat dither-r until I pr-romised I'd no har-rm yon cow that hor-rned her-r. No doubt she's daft wi' pain.'

" 'Well, Father,' I said, 'I can't give an opinion about Mother until I've examined her. And I think you'd better not go along into her room when I do—you're hiding a great dither, yourself. I'll let you know what I find as soon as I can.' His face working, Father turned away and walked towards the orchard.

"Near the kitchen door, I paused beside a pile of cord-wood to breathe in the fragrance of new chips around the chopping block. Then I walked over to a great cast-iron kettle squatting on short tripod legs over a dead fire. The kettle was three-quarters full of half-made soap. My sister,

Bertie, came to the door and said, 'Hello, Rab,' then noticed me looking at the kettle, and explained: 'Mother was
making soap when the cow gored her. I've the kitchen table
laid, Rab. We made barley soup against your coming,' she
smiled.

" 'So you remembered, Bertie, how much I like barley
soup,' I said.

" 'No, it was Mother who remembered,' she said.

"Mother and her barley soup! How I'd loved it as a boy!
Thick and meaty, it was. I liked it best with slices of bread
spread thick with apple butter. Apple butter! I looked again
at the huge black kettle, and instead of the soap, saw it, in
memory, filled with bubbling apple butter, and Mother stir-
ring with a big wooden paddle. Bushel baskets grouped close
by were heaped with Northern spies, yellow mellows, brown,
rough-skinned russets, small, bright-red snowapples. Beside
them, a hogshead of newly-pressed cider. The autumn air
was redolent with cinnamon, cloves and the smoke from
burning hickory, oak and pine chips. My mother wore a
blue-and-white checked apron.

"The vision faded, and I realized Mother, hurt and brok-
en, was waiting for me. I went into the house, walked
through the kitchen where Dr. McLeod, Nurse McLean and
my brothers were eating, and entered Mother's bedroom.
Tiny and drawn, with closed eyes, she lay in the big double
bed that she and Father'd shared for more than forty years.
Dr. Townsend, the 'new' doctor, was standing beside a window.

" 'She's awake, Doctor,' he said.

"Mother opened her eyes. 'Ye've come, laddie,' she whispered. Then anxiously: 'Ye'll no be lettin' them har-rm yon
beastie that butted me, Rab. Th' poor-r cr-reatur-re was fair-r
demented wi' a bee sting. Pr-romise . . .'

" 'Dinna fash yer-rsel', Mither-r,' I said, growing Scotsy

with emotion. 'Th' beast'll no be har-rmed.' I kissed her and
she closed her eyes.

"I examined her slowly, and carefully, then said to Dr.
Townsend:

" 'I'll operate.'

"Mother opened her eyes and tried to smile. 'Let it be in
th' butter-ry, then, laddie,' she said.

"The buttery! Yes—Mother's prayer room, with its clean
freshness—the long table beneath the whitewash-frosted windows!

"I nodded to Dr. Townsend. 'Tell Dr. McLeod and Nurse
McLean to make things ready in the buttery at once.' I
watched the young doctor leave the room, then sat in a chair
to hide a sudden trembling.

"As I sat looking at Mother, apparently asleep, I realized
with sudden panic that this trembling was psychological—
probably stemming from a childhood fear of seeing Mother
hurt. I willed the trembling to stop. Instead, it grew worse.
I called Bertie to come and stay with Mother, then pausing
at the buttery door only long enough to see the two doctors
and Nurse McLean rapidly turning it into an operating
room, I walked outside.

"I rested my shaking hands on the piled cordwood, flexing
the fingers, trying to still a mounting obsession that if I
operated, I'd fail. I tried to rationalize my condition, telling
myself I was a mature man—an experienced surgeon. It
didn't help. I continued to feel very young and very frightened.

"From the kitchen doorway, Dr. Townsend called, 'Ready
now, Dr. Lindsey.'

" 'In a moment, Dr. Townsend,' I said, and silently cried
to God for steadiness and quick perception.

"As I stood savoring an immediate in-pouring of faith, I
noted vaguely that my brothers were ploughing and harrow-

ing a distant clover field; that Father was standing, hands clasped behind him, looking up at an oriole's nest that hung from the one live, blossom-laden branch of an old russet apple tree. I walked out to him and told him I was certain that all would go well.

" 'I believe, Rabbie, I believe,' he said.

"With the trembling gone, and a deep feeling of confidence, I went into the kitchen, drank a cup of hot soup, scrubbed-up at the sink, then stepped into the buttery. Mother, covered with a white sheet, smiled at me drowsily. I put my fingers on her pulse, and nodded to Dr. McLeod to begin anesthesia.

"It was a long, difficult operation—one that presented several intricate problems—surgery that would have resulted fatally had I made a single mistake. Yet it went smoothly— perfectly. Never before had I worked with such skill and assurance."

"You dressed her, and God healed her," I said.

"Yes," Dr. Lindsey agreed. "And that's the way it's been ever since—I 'dress' them, and God heals them."

*I*DLING *in the lobby of a small-town hotel in Northern California a few months ago, I picked up the local newspaper and read:*

PRAYERS AID CURE OF MENTAL ILLS; SAYS FORMER PATIENT

The story said briefly that Mrs. Lois Amherst, a housewife who'd undergone treatment for mental illness at Agnews State Hospital, had spoken to the local women's club about her experience, and among other things, had declared that prayers can help physicians achieve quick, permanent cures.

A few weeks later, in another small town, I read in its newspaper:

PRAYER PLUS THERAPY CURE FOR MIND ILLNESS

Again, the story concerned Lois Amherst, and her talk to a local women's group. When, two months later, I read a third, and similar newspaper story about Mrs. Amherst, I called her at her home near Santa Cruz. When I told her I was a collector of prayer stories, she said:

"If you can come to our home this evening, my husband and I will tell you the story together."

So I talked with the Amhersts. The result is "Through the Valley of the Shadow."

Through the Valley of the Shadow

HAD RALPH AND LOIS Amherst been able to recognize soon enough the early symptoms of mental illness, they could have prevented their world from tumbling about their ears. Had their attitude toward mental sickness been the same as their attitude toward physical sickness, they'd have escaped months of humiliation and despair. And even a partial understanding of the marvelous advances made in techniques of treating mental disorders would have saved them near financial bankruptcy.

But the Amhersts—like millions of other Americans—looked on mental illness as something disgraceful—something almost criminal. In most ways, the Amhersts were an admirable couple. They read good books, good magazines, were well-educated, owned their own home, attended churches, were active in the P.T.A.; had been married for fifteen years, and had never fallen out of love with each other. Both had read numerous articles on mental hygiene, and in a vague way, both knew that mental health was a major national problem. But the idea that mental illness might strike in their own family had never consciously entered their heads. Their attitude toward families of two acquaintances who'd suffered mental breakdowns was sympathetic, yet in a man-

234

ner somewhat similar to their sympathy for the family of a neighbor who'd been imprisoned for a crime.

The Amhersts had two children, Harold, fourteen, and Mary, ten, and were rearing them in a manner tending to teach them responsibility for the results of their own behavior. The family was kindly—kind to others, kind to one another. Ralph, forty-eight, was an accountant, with his office in his home. Lois, forty-two, was his assistant. Ralph was energetic, inclined to be excitable. Lois was calm and deliberate. The atmosphere of their home and their office was one of quiet happiness.

Then, early in June 1950, Lois went through two days and nights of deep depression, during which she spoke hardly at all. This dark mood was followed by a full day during which she was filled with happy excitement. She said to Ralph:

"I don't know what I'm so pepped-up about, but I feel as if something wonderful's going to happen."

The following two weeks, Lois was her usual, serene self. Then came two more days of depression, resentment towards visitors; impatience towards Ralph and the children. Again, optimistic excitement returned, this time so strong that she was unable to sleep. She walked about all one night, singing softly to herself—smiling occasionally at inward, happy thoughts.

In July, when the children were away on vacation, Lois began speaking disparagingly of Ralph, and of his work. Only slightly perturbed, Ralph shrugged this off. However, when Lois—who'd seldom spoken ill of anyone—became severely critical of nearly everybody, Ralph protested. Lois replied, "If you knew what I know about these people, you'd feel antagonistic too, Ralph. You think they're your friends. They're not—they're only using you."

"Lois!" Ralph said.

"You think you understand people," Lois said, "but you

don't. You got your knowledge from books, and the books are wrong."

"Wrong?"

"Yes, wrong. We don't need books. There's a better way to acquire knowledge."

"Through experience, you mean?" Ralph asked doubtfully.

"Don't bother me, Ralph," Lois said impatiently. "No—I don't mean 'through experience.' There's no use trying to tell you how, for you wouldn't be able to understand." She returned to her work at a ledger; sat with pen in hand, turning pages, making notes. Ralph, also working on accounts, glanced at her from time to time, with troubled eyes.

Supper-time came and passed, and still Lois sat, absorbed. Finally Ralph said, "Why don't you knock off work now, darling? You look tired. I'll whip up something to eat."

"Don't bother me, Ralph," Lois said absently. "I've got to get this job done tonight."

"Why tonight, darling? We've two weeks to audit that account."

"If you don't leave me alone, Ralph, I'll scream. This job *has* to be done tonight. It's far more important than you seem to think. I'd tell you why, but you'd not understand."

Lois's face was drawn, her eyes too bright. Ralph put a hand on her shoulder and said:

"Please, darling, stop now, and rest. You're driving yourself beyond reason. There's nothing really important about that account. It can . . ."

Lois looked at Ralph with sudden hatred, and said, "You think you're my boss, Ralph, but you aren't. I'm not working for you. It's true that you hired me, but you can't fire me. I have orders from my real boss. Now please stop pestering me." She turned back to the ledger.

Both shocked, and hurt, Ralph waited in the living room

until past midnight when Lois finally emerged from the office.

"Well, that's done, and I'm very tired," she said, and went to her room without even a smile.

Ralph walked into the office and looked at the ledger she'd worked on so hard and so long. *She'd not made a single entry in it.* He looked at the notes she'd left beside the ledger. They concerned 'filing by colors,' and Ralph could make nothing of them.

Early next morning, Lois returned to work at the same ledger, and at her notes. Ralph went downtown on a business errand, and when he returned, handed her a book, and told her, "I ran across this in the bookstore downtown— *The Garden of the Prophet.* Thought you'd like it."

With an expression of annoyance, Lois tossed the book aside and said: "I don't need books any more, Ralph."

Ralph smiled.

"Don't laugh," she went on angrily.

"Doggone it, darling," Ralph said. "I'm not laughing. I didn't mean to offend you. I thought . . ."

"All knowledge comes from the air," Lois said. "All one needs to do is to learn to contact it. I've been tuning-in on it, Ralph, and I've learned something. And now it's time you knew it. You must get away—get out of this county quickly. You mustn't let them catch you."

"Catch me! Who?"

"The police are after you. They're on their way to get you now. They're coming in cars, and they're honking horns."

"Lois! What the . . . ?"

Lois pushed her chair back, got to her feet and said coldly:

"I'm going to my room, Ralph. I don't want to be here when the police arrive."

Ralph Amherst stared after his wife—fear in his eyes. Feeling almost physically sick himself, he telephoned Dr.

Clifton Ayers, a psychiatrist, and asked him to come to their home at once. He met Ayers at the door, took him into the office, shut the door and told what had been happening.

Dr. Ayers said, "Mrs. Amherst's condition must have been coming on for a long while. You've just not recognized it. You say she doesn't sleep well recently?"

"Very little. She prowls the house, picks things up, puts them down again. Sometimes she stands listening intently. She's been taking sleeping pills for some time, but they seem to be losing their effect."

"Bring her in here to the office, Mr. Amherst," Dr. Ayers said.

Lois spoke from her bedroom doorway. "I told you to get away, Ralph, but you've paid no attention. I'll talk to the officer."

"Lois," Ralph said gently, "there's no officer. Come and meet Clifton Ayers, a doctor." He walked with her into the office, and she looked at Dr. Ayers.

"How silly can you get, Ralph?" she said. "This man's no doctor—he's a policeman. He's from the FBI. She told me he was coming here."

"She? Who, Lois?"

"Mrs. Roosevelt told me."

"Oh, God, darling!" Ralph said, and walked blindly from the room.

For an hour, Dr. Ayers talked with Lois, then called to Ralph to bring the sleeping pills. The doctor gave Lois three tablets, watched her grow drowsy and finally fall asleep on the office studio couch. Ralph covered her with a blanket, then accompanied Dr. Ayers to his car. From behind the wheel, Dr. Ayers said:

"When Mrs. Amherst wakens, she'll be either much calmer, or very much worse. In either case, I advise that you commit her to a state mental hospital—Agnews. And the sooner, the better—tomorrow morning. She's suffering a common form of mental illness, Mr. Amherst. For want of a better term, we call it 'menopausal psychosis.' She needs special therapy—she *must* have it."

"Agnews!" Ralph's face went white.

"Don't take this too hard, Amherst. Our state mental hospitals are among the finest in the land."

"Do you mean, Doctor, that Lois is insane? Is that it?"

"No—certainly not. She's mentally and emotionally ill— is even affected physically already. With proper therapy, she'll probably be well and home again within six months."

"But Agnews! An insane asylum!"

"Insane asylum, Amherst, is a term held over from the dark ages," Dr. Ayers explained. "In California, in New York, Michigan, Massachusetts—in many of our more advanced states, there are *no* insane asylums, as you call them. We have mental hospitals in which the finest physicians in the world cure eighty-five per cent of all cases such as Mrs. Amherst's." He started his car. "You'd better go in now, Amherst, and keep an eye on your wife. If she wakens in bad shape, telephone and I'll come right out."

"WELL," RALPH AMHERST SAID to me as he, Mrs. Amherst and I sat on the porch of their home, "I sat all that night at our dining room table, listening for sounds from the office, repeating over and over: 'This can't be happening!'

"Once I tiptoed into the room, saw Lois apparently asleep, and turned to leave. She spoke, and with eyes still closed, said:

" 'I see you, Ralph. You're a black shadow surrounded by green, diffused light.'

"In the morning she seemed almost her old, usual self. She

kept busy with housework while I worked in the office.
Around noon, I telephoned Dr. Ayers and said, 'Lois seems
perfectly normal, Doctor. She's washing dishes right now,
and singing. Don't you think this means she's going to be all
right, after all?'

" 'No, Amherst. I think this is only another phase. If I
were you, I'd get her to the hospital now, while she's cooperative.'

" 'But she seems so perfectly normal, Doctor. I certainly
don't want to . . .' I heard Lois moan. 'Hold the line,
Doctor,' I said. I dropped the receiver and rushed to the
kitchen. Lois was wringing her hands, and crying. She said
hysterically:

" 'The children, Ralph! They're in danger. Find them,
quickly! Bring them in the house! Quickly, Ralph! They're
in awful danger!'

" 'Darling! The kids are on vacation,' I said. 'They're in
no danger! What in the world makes you think they're in
danger?'

" 'That horn! That auto horn! Didn't you hear it, Ralph?
It's a warning. That car's hunting for the children to hurt
them—maybe kill them!' She clutched my arm and cried
wildly: 'Bring them in the house, Ralph! Quickly!'

"I went back to the telephone. 'Doctor,' I said, 'you'd better come right out. She's in an awful state.'

" 'I'll come at once,' Dr. Ayers said quietly, and hung up
the receiver.

"When the doctor arrived, I told him of Lois's fears for
the children, of what she thought was the portent of auto
horns. Oblivious to all but her fantasies, Lois paced the floor,
wringing her hands, mumbling incoherently.

"Dr. Ayers took one of her hands and said firmly, 'You're
not helping your children by acting this way, Mrs. Amherst.

If they're really in danger, you should be *doing* something about it instead of acting like a frightened child.'

"Lois looked at him quite sanely. 'What can I do?' she asked meekly.

" 'Well,' Dr. Ayers said, 'for one thing, you can let me take you to a hospital. You're ill, Mrs. Amherst. And while you're in the hospital, the children will be safe. I give you my word.'

"Lois stared long and hard at the doctor, then said:

" 'I know a lot more of what's going on than you think I do. You and Ralph think I'm crazy. You want to put me away.' She put her fingers to her mouth thoughtfully, then said uncertainly: 'But I'm not crazy. Am I? Am I?'

" 'Of course you're not,' Dr. Ayers said, 'but you're at the point of breakdown. You must have hospital treatment.'

"Lois laughed, then said, 'You aren't fooling me—you're a policeman. You've come for Ralph. And I know why, too— because Ralph's responsible for the Korean War. Ralph's sinned, so the war came. But only I can stop it. Listen!' she said tensely. 'Hear the horns? Can you hear the horns?' Her eyes held panic. 'The bells!' she said in a whisper, 'do you hear the bells?' She began to pace the floor again.

" 'Let her pace, Mr. Amherst,' the doctor said to me, 'but don't let her leave the house. I'll call Agnews Hospital and make arrangements.' He started towards the telephone.

" 'Not Agnews, Doctor!' I said. 'I can't let her . . .' I broke off, looked at Lois, then said:

" 'Call a private sanitarium, Doctor—a good one.'

"Dr. Ayers hesitated, and said, 'You're not a wealthy man, Mr. Amherst. Private sanitariums are expensive.'

" 'I don't care what it costs,' I said, 'I'll get the money somehow.'

" 'But Agnews State Hospital is well equipped, Amherst— has capable doctors and technicians.'

" 'No,' I said. 'Call it what you like, it's still an insane asylum. Oh, God, Doctor, don't argue with me.'

"So Dr. Ayers went to the telephone and called a private sanitarium.

"A FEW HOURS LATER that day, looking helpless and forlorn, Lois was led away from the office of the private mental institution by two white-clad nurses. I followed her with my eyes until she entered a building across a roadway.

" 'Shall we take care of the business arrangements now, please, Mr. Amherst?' a voice said. I looked at the woman who'd spoken, nodded and took out my checkbook.

" 'The rate is two hundred dollars a week—in advance, Mr. Amherst,' she said.

" 'How long will Mrs. Amherst be here, do you think?' I asked hopefully.

" 'I'm sure I don't know,' she said. 'Perhaps you'd better make your check for three months. That'll be $2,400.'

"I wrote the check for eight hundred dollars. 'I'll see how she is at the end of four weeks,' I said.

" 'Just as you wish,' the woman said, then added with a smile: 'Almost all of our patients are from wealthy families, of course, Mr. Amherst.'

"Lois improved steadily, and remained at the sanitarium until I ran out of money. When I told the head doctor I wanted to take her home, he wouldn't hear of it. I said, 'But she wants to go home; our youngsters are home now; we all want her home.'

" 'Mrs. Amherst is coming along fine,' the doctor said, 'but she needs a lot more therapy. I feel it imperative that you keep her here for another two months, at least.'

" 'But I've run out of money, Doctor,' I said.

" 'Oh,' he said. 'Well, in that case . . .'

"LOIS WAS SO HAPPY to be at home again, and seemed so normal that I believed she was permanently well. However, Dr. Ayers didn't think so.

" 'She should have many more electric shock treatments,' he told me. 'Take her to Agnews for them. Their equipment is modern; electric shock equipment at the private hospital was far out-moded.'

"That evening I discussed Agnews with Lois, and she said:

" 'I only want to do what's right, Ralph. I want to be completely well again for all four of our sakes—I think you know that. But please, dear, let me have a few more days here at home—only a few more, darling.'

"And three days later, Lois began hearing horns and bells again. She was more erratic than she'd ever been before. She opened every water faucet in the house, insisted on keeping them running. 'Water *must* flow,' she explained, 'if the Korean War is to stop.' Then she began lighting matches and holding them high above her head. 'They're sacrifices for the poor soldiers who've died, Ralph—who can never have any more babies,' she said. When very early one morning, she put on her fur coat, picked up her typewriter, walked out of the house—in stockinged feet—and started down the street, I went after her, bundled her into the car and drove her to Agnews.

"While Lois was being treated there," Ralph said, "I met many of Agnews' doctors, nurses and attendants. And never have I seen professional people more overworked, more weary at night, yet more eager to help. And let me add, never have I known professional people paid so poorly in proportion to their abilities and achievements. Well," he went on after a short pause, "the rest of Lois's story can best be told by her." He looked at her adoringly. "Carry on, soldier," he said.

"I'VE NO RECOLLECTION at all of entering Agnews," Lois began, "and I've no memories of the first eight days. I was told, however, that I was kept in a tepid bath of running water almost continuously for three days in the hope it would soothe my nerves sufficiently to let me sleep. It didn't work, so they finally tried electric shock—which did.

"Sometime during the ninth day I began to realize vaguely that I was in a bed, apparently in a hospital. I asked a nurse what was wrong with me. She said, with a kindly hand on my arm:

" 'You've had a mental upset, my dear. You're at Agnews Hospital. We're going to help you get well.'

"I remember saying, 'That's nice of you,' then turned away from the nurse, puzzled about the word 'Agnews.' The word seemed familiar, but I couldn't place it. I don't remember anything more of that day, but on the morning of the tenth day, another nurse said to me:

" 'Today is the day of your hearing, Mrs. Amherst. The doctors want to be sure that you really need treatment. In California, you know, no one's officially committed to a state mental institution without a hearing.'

"I was physically very weak that day, but my mind felt clear. 'Will my husband be at the hearing?' I asked.

"When told that he would be, I said, 'Then it'll be all right. Have I been troublesome, Nurse?'

" 'A little,' she smiled, 'but that's all over now.'

"In the hearing room, three doctors who had no connection with state institutions sat at one side of a long table. A stenographer sat at one end. Six nurses sat in a row along one wall. Ralph and I were seated side-by-side, opposite the doctors. Ralph held my hand. Said one doctor:

" 'We're about to question you, Mrs. Amherst, to find out whether or not you should be officially committed to Agnews. Those six nurses are a jury. This is California's way of pro-

tecting you against illegal commitment. Do you understand
what I'm saying?'

" 'Yes,' I answered.

"They then asked Ralph to describe my actions from the
first day he'd noticed that I'd seemed mentally disturbed.
When he'd finished, they questioned me. I wasn't frightened
—the doctors were all kind men, and the jury of nurses
seemed friendly. I answered some questions with difficulty,
for my mind now seemed very slow. The rest of the hearing
is vague—I remember that the three doctors signed papers,
and I remember Ralph kissing me just before a nurse led
me away. The next thing I remember is wakening in a bed
in a ward with many other women. Later, after a breakfast
of cereal, stewed fruit, a hard-boiled egg, bread, butter, milk
and coffee, I walked over to a large window and stood looking out at green lawns and trees. I felt lonely and frightened.
A car drove past, and I caught myself listening for the sound
of its horn. I thought of Mary and Harold, prayed silently
that they'd be safe, then began crying softly.

"A kind voice said, 'Good morning, Mrs. Amherst.'

"I looked around at the speaker—a calm, motherly woman
with a friendly smile and steady, warm, thoughtful eyes. She
wore a long white professional coat.

" 'I'm Dr. Jean Swain,' she said, 'and you're going to be
my patient for a while.'

" 'Do you think you can make me well, Doctor?' I asked.

" 'I'm sure we can, but that depends largely on you too,'
she said.

" 'On me?'

" 'Yes, Mrs. Amherst—on your cooperation with us. Try
to accept treatments with good grace—try to keep in mind
that our goal, and our greatest joy is to see patients leave
us well again both in mind and in body.'

" 'Am I going to have more shock treatments?'

" 'Yes—quite a lot of them. But you've had them before, and you know they're painless.'

" 'But I dread them so, Doctor. I always feel so lost afterwards. Sometimes it's hours before I can remember anything.'

" 'But you usually sleep better on nights following shock treatments, don't you? They're a part of our program to make you well—and that's why you're here, Lois.'

' 'Will I be here long?'

" 'Not very long—only as long as you need to be,' she smiled. She patted my shoulder and moved on to another patient.

"I leaned my hot forehead against the cool window pane. With all the intensity of my troubled heart, I cried silently:

" 'Oh, please, God, help me to cooperate. Help me, God, to get well soon and go home to my darlings.'

"From that moment on, through the bad days or nights— through the good days or nights—a small prayer, 'God, guide me and guard me,' was ever in my mind and heart. That short phrase became my life-line.

"With each additional shock treatment, my mind became less confused. I was now better able to enjoy and appreciate —even to answer—the many cheering and helpful letters, cards and small gifts that came to me from friends, relatives and neighbors. Time after time when despair threatened, those messages gave me courage to fight on. I truly believe that kindly, newsy letters are one of the most important aids in mental therapy. How often I longed to comfort those whose families and friends seldom wrote them.

"After about twelve shock treatments, I began taking an interest in other patients in the wards. I listened to their troubles, hopes, fears, dreams. While each had individual worries, there was one that was common to all—a dread of going home to face friends and neighbors who might consider mental illness a stigma.

"I noticed that this fear of what people might think or say was greater among women of farms and small towns. It's in isolated, rural communities, more so than in cities, that the old ignorance-fostered attitudes and superstitions regarding mental illness hold sway.

"I knew exactly how many of my fellow-patients dreaded facing old neighbors, for I, too, had cringed at the thought of meeting mine.

"However, my own dread vanished when I learned that almost every family has some member or relative who's undergone psychiatric or institutional treatment for mental ills.

"For some time, I'd prayed God would show me how best to use my hospital experiences for the good of others. One afternoon the answer came. A rainbow appeared in the sky outside my ward. In unison, all patients immediately crowded our windows to look at it. The rainbow was a happy omen to all, and as I glanced from the rainbow to all the rapt faces, my heart went out to each. I longed to do something to help. In a flash I had an answer to my prayer:

"I'd visit small towns and rural communities, telling the true story of mental hospitals—telling my own story—doing what I could to dispel fears, myths and fallacies concerning mental health.

"And with a new song in my heart, I watched the rainbow fade.

"After twelve more electric shock treatments, I was released from Agnews. I said goodbye to patients, nurses, technicians, and to the three doctors who'd given me such unstinting care—Doctors Jean Swain, Louise Abrahams, and Kristian Johnsen."

Lois reached over and put her hand on Ralph's. "And so I came home," she said.

"Yes," Ralph said softly, "she came home—and it meant that a whole family had found its soul again."

As I prepared to leave, the Amhersts stood up and shook hands. Lois said:

"If you write my story, please say that I now know that had I taken my original frustrations and anxieties to God in prayer, they'd never have accumulated to that point beyond bearing. Since my mental hospital experiences, I've talked to many leading psychologists, and each said that most people who take their daily problems to God in prayer, and who follow His guidance, never need a psychiatrist's help.

"Every mental hospital doctor to whom I've talked has said that patients who pray are the most cooperative ones, and that consequently, complete cure comes comparatively soon to them.

"And please," Lois said earnestly, "quote Dr. James T. Fisher, the noted psychiatrist, who wrote:

"*If you were to take the sum total of all the authoritative articles ever written by the most qualified of psychologists and psychiatrists on the subject of mental hygiene, if you were to combine them and refine them and cleave out the excess verbiage, if you were to take the whole of the meat and none of the parsley, and if you were to have these unadulterated bits of pure scientific knowledge concisely expressed by the most capable of living poets, you would have an awkward and incomplete summation of the Sermon on the Mount.*" [1]

---

[1] James T. Fisher, M.D., *A Few Buttons Missing; The Case Book of a Psychiatrist,* written in collaboration with Lowell S. Hawley (Lippincott).